Elizabeth's Song

One Family's Journey through Autism

DR. DAVID A. BISHOP

WESTBOW
PRESS®
A DIVISION OF THOMAS NELSON
& ZONDERVAN

The information, ideas, and suggestions in this book are not intended as a substitute for professional medical advice. Before following any suggestions contained in this book, you should consult your personal physician. Neither the author nor the publisher shall be liable or responsible for any loss or damage allegedly arising as a consequence of your use or application of any information or suggestions in this book.

WestBow Press books may be ordered through booksellers or by contacting:

WestBow Press
A Division of Thomas Nelson & Zondervan
1663 Liberty Drive
Bloomington, IN 47403
www.westbowpress.com
1 (866) 928-1240

Because of the dynamic nature of the Internet, any web addresses or links contained in this book may have changed since publication and may no longer be valid. The views expressed in this work are solely those of the author and do not necessarily reflect the views of the publisher, and the publisher hereby disclaims any responsibility for them.

Unless otherwise stated, scripture quotations are from the ESV® Bible (The Holy Bible, English Standard Version®), copyright © 2001 by Crossway, a publishing ministry of Good News Publishers. Used by permission. All rights reserved.

Scripture quotations marked (NIV) are taken from the Holy Bible, New International Version®, NIV®. Copyright © 1973, 1978, 1984, 2011 by Biblica, Inc.™ Used by permission of Zondervan. All rights reserved worldwide. www.zondervan.com The "NIV" and "New International Version" are trademarks registered in the United States Patent and Trademark Office by Biblica, Inc.™

ISBN: 978-1-9736-2409-7 (sc)
ISBN: 978-1-9736-2408-0 (hc)
ISBN: 978-1-9736-2410-3 (e)

Library of Congress Control Number: 2018903696

Print information available on the last page.

WestBow Press rev. date: 4/30/2018

To my wife, Deborah, and my beautiful daughter, Elizabeth Dorothy.

Contents

Introduction
Why I Wrote This Book

If you have picked up this book, chances are good that you or someone you love has autism. Autism is a condition that affects as many as one in eighty children; it is approaching epidemic proportions. Autism is a complex neurobiological condition that lasts a lifetime, affecting a person's ability to communicate and relate to others. Referred to as Autism Spectrum Disorder (ASD), the condition's severity can vary widely, from very mild to extremely debilitating. At the same time, resources to support parents and children coping with the condition fall far short of what is needed. Educational, medical, and insurance support are often inadequate or completely nonexistent. Being primarily classified as a mental condition, autism does not get the attention, coverage, or support that other problems do. Although it affects more children than HIV, diabetes, and pediatric cancer combined, autism has far less research funding, community support, and medical assistance than each of those conditions. Even though autism is becoming more commonplace, the public at large still poorly understands it. This is all changing for the better, but progress is slow.

Autism is a tough row to hoe because it often makes you feel as though everyone has failed you. As a parent or relative of an autistic child, you may feel the whole world is against you—your doctors fail you, teachers and educators fail you, the legal system fails you, and sometimes it feels as if your own family fails you. There have been times when my wife and I were at our wits' end. Working to make sure your child is getting the best therapy, medical care, and educational assistance in addition to dealing with the day-to-day struggles of managing autism can be exhausting. With a condition that is poorly understood by even the experts, the unknowns can make it very difficult to determine if you are doing the best for your child. Our minds often swirled with questions: Is this the right therapy? Is this the best medical approach? Is this the best school? What are the teachers really doing with our child daily? Are we trained well enough to deal with the problems at home? Is our child progressing or regressing? What will happen as our child gets older? Is our child eating enough? What caused this? Was it our fault? These questions can eat away at you to the point of making yourself physically ill.

As I researched, I found that many parents in our situation were so beleaguered they had begun questioning their faith. I wrote this book for them, for you. I'm here to tell you that no matter how bad things get, there is a light at the end of the tunnel. There *is* joy to be had in your life with your child. God does have a plan, a destination. But getting there sometimes takes a little help and understanding—understanding that you may not be getting from anyone else, that can only be found with others who have had the same experiences. As a result, to make this book as valuable to you as possible, I have not pulled any punches. I'm sharing with you the raw feelings and experiences that any parent in this position would. If I didn't, my account would appear fake, as if I didn't really experience what you are experiencing or as if I didn't have it "quite as bad," thereby invalidating my advice. No, my story is real, my friend. I'm sharing this experience with you in the hopes that you will not only find some good advice for dealing with common problems associated with autism but that it will also give you comfort and hope.

1

The Happiest Day of My Life

Behold, children are a heritage from the Lord, the fruit of the womb a reward.

—Psalm 127:3

D ebbie and I had always wanted children. It was in our plan. We had visions of two—a boy and a girl—although we would have been happy with whatever God provided. During the early years of our marriage, we just let things flow naturally, without any kind of timeline. We spent the first few years getting to know each other, traveling, and experiencing life.

However, we had both hit thirty by the time we were married, and time flies fast. Unfortunately, our bodies have only so much time to produce healthy children. This is particularly true with women. Although women can certainly have children well into their forties, doctors typically consider their pregnancies high-risk once they're over thirty-five. By the time we reached our midthirties, we began to have some concern and decided to have ourselves checked.

At first, due to our insurance restrictions, we had to go through several steps and tests before any action could be taken. The HMO made my wife in particular step through one test after another, most of which were inconclusive or ambiguous: "Well, there could be an issue here, but we have to run yet another test."

After we had exhausted the HMO process, the gynecologist was able to give us a referral to a reproductive specialist, who turned out to be a fantastic doctor. This guy really knew his stuff. He was blunt and direct, but he got things fixed quickly. I had some pain myself, which he fixed with a ten-second suggestion. He then checked my wife and found that she had a polyp in her uterus that needed to be removed. It was keeping fertilized eggs from sticking to her uterine wall.

After a relatively simply laparoscopy to remove it, the doctor told us we'd be pregnant in about three months. I highly doubted him. *Really? I thought. How could he give such a guarantee?* But sure enough, by the third month, my wife noticed that her period had stopped for a while. She thought nothing of it at first, because it wasn't entirely unusual for her to be late. But when she took a pregnancy test, we were delighted. We did it twice just to be sure. I still remember the disbelief in my wife's eyes. I'd never seen them bug out like that. We were both so happy. Getting pregnant isn't easy for everyone, and for those who have struggled, it is indeed a very exciting and joyful event. So many people take for granted the gift of a new life.

During the next few months, we prepared as any new parents would by getting the nursery together, buying clothes and toys, and preparing for the big day. Debbie's pregnancy was relatively uneventful, with no real problems or concerns.

Debbie's pregnancy ran a bit late, and she was eventually induced. I was apprehensive about the process but also somewhat relieved that we could plan our birth without having to undergo the stress of racing to the hospital.

I opted to sit in on the birth of our daughter. It was truly the happiest and most exhilarating moment of my life. Watching a live birth is like nothing else. Excitement, tension, happiness, and fear are all present in the room. The doctor and nurse watched me like a hawk as I tried to comfort my wife. They seemed to be keeping as much of an eye on me as they were her. They thought I would pass out or vomit at the scene, and honestly I had to close my eyes a bit during part of it.

When Elizabeth left her mother's womb, they cleaned her up and weighed her as I watched. They then let me hold her for the first time. She was beautiful. I most remember her ears. They were small and just a bit floppy, like kittens' ears when they are born.

The flood of emotions that a parent feels at the birth of a child, especially his or her first, is like no other. It is sometimes difficult to explain this to people who are not parents. The truth that no one really reveals is that you don't truly become human until you have had a child. Having children is a major, if not the most definitive, part of the human experience. If you haven't had a child, you have not experienced what it's really like to be human. You haven't experienced a key part of life, and I don't believe you really mature as a person. Having a child changes the way you think and look at life. It also floods you with the most powerful emotions you'll ever experience. The love you have for that child will be greater than any love you will ever know. A switch will flip in your brain, and if you're like most people, you change.

Sadly, many of our friends have put money and success above having children. They are so worried about keeping up with the Joneses that they have lost perspective on what life is all about. They compensate with animals or material pursuits. I love animals too, but they aren't human beings, and using them as surrogates just doesn't work. Perhaps I'm being too judgmental. After all, people have the right to pursue happiness in their own ways, to find their own paths. To get the most out of life, however, I believe God's path is the best.

Oh, the joy my little girl gave me that day. I was filled with love like no other. Let me say this while it's on my mind: Although our little girl has special needs, we have no regrets. I would still have her again. I love her just as she is. She has her own personality, her own self. She shows love to us in her own way, and I'm blessed and enriched every day by it. Some of our selfish friends look at us with a sigh of relief that they didn't have children. Others think we are jealous of families of typical children because our child is not "normal." Nothing could be more ignorant. Elizabeth has changed me, my wife, and our lives for the better. She has enriched us to no end and made us better people. She teaches us lessons every day, and we constantly learn and grow from her. She has made us stronger and better people, and we are convinced that it's all part of God's plan for her and for us to move on to bigger challenges.

For Elizabeth's birth, we had decided to go to the downtown hospital known as the "baby hospital." We'd heard all sorts of good things about the facilities. We wanted to be sure our child was right in the center of the best care available, should any problems arise. However, we didn't feel very comfortable once we got there. I had some concerns about the antibiotic that our daughter was given as a precaution against a supposed infection. In retrospect, I thought maybe the country hospital near us would have been a better choice. However, those worries seemed to melt away every time I looked at my beautiful baby girl.

Lessons Learned

1. Have children if you can. You are missing out on a big part of life if you don't.
2. Don't let people put you on *their* timeline. Go by *yours*. My wife's first gynecologist kept telling her to keep trying for three to four years before undergoing any tests. When you are thirty-five years old, that just doesn't make sense. Her second gynecologist told her to wait a year or two for our second child. This caused us not to have one. Again, go by your timeline and God's—not anyone else's.
3. If your insurance or medical provider puts barriers in front of you, move through the hoops as fast as you can so you can see a decent reproductive specialist.
4. Go to the hospital where you feel most comfortable. There's no such thing as the "best baby hospital."
5. Understand that God's wisdom is infinite and that he has a plan. Have faith.

2

Signs

After we brought Elizabeth home, she seemed completely normal. Her Apgar scores in the hospital were good. She was already lifting her head and rolling over within the first week of life. She had a brief episode of reflux, which stopped once her milk was cut back. We learned about the "back to sleep" campaign, which encourages parents to have their babies sleep on their backs, due to unexplained deaths from SIDS (sudden infant death syndrome). Being dutiful parents, we put her on a special pad that encouraged her to sleep on her back.

We got set up with a pediatrician who was approved through our insurance and began regular visits. As most typically do, the pediatrician pushed additional vaccines, including flu and rotavirus vaccines. She also pushed us to get the hepatitis B vaccine, which I had previously turned down at the hospital. I eventually relented.

One thing I need to say about pediatricians, which is pretty simple advice but should never be taken lightly, is this: do your research. Get recommendations from friends, family, and neighbors. Do an internet search on the doctor and even a background check, if you can. If something doesn't feel right when you go there, turn around and leave. It's easy when you have a new baby, especially if it's your first one, to get so excited you forget to do all of this due diligence. My advice to you is this: *don't forget.* Slow down. Take your time in selecting a pediatrician, and don't hesitate to change if there's something bothering you. The pediatrician you select, if you select well, will be with you and your family for many years. Take the time to pick the one who is best for you.

In our case, I had different insurance at the time, which limited our choices. I went to a single-doctor practice without doing much research. The office was not terribly far from home and was easily accessible from my job. From the first appointment, there were things that bothered me. During each visit, I was always surprised that we were the only ones in the waiting room. The doctor seemed okay but was often dismissive of most issues we brought forward. Once the assistant said she was giving Elizabeth a shot that I thought was different from what the doctor had just told us she was getting. There was an ensuing argument outside the room, and that assistant was later fired. We were never told anything, but I have always wondered and worried about that incident. After finally doing some research online, I found that there had been several serious complaints about this doctor. After about eighteen months, we switched to a good pediatrician in a larger multi-doctor practice that was just down the road from our house. I was dumbfounded that we had not discovered this doctor sooner, but I had focused on what my insurance recommended. By the time we changed doctors, I had changed jobs and had better coverage.

Elizabeth had problems sitting up and would not tolerate staying on her stomach very much. We tried all sorts of "tummy time" techniques and devices with no real results. Later, she seemed to turn her head to the side. Her first pediatrician said she had some torticollis and recommended physical therapy. Torticollis is basically where the neck is strained, and although the doctor suggested that this happened in the womb, I wondered if it really happened during birth when the obstetrician was extricating her. Things like this they never tell you, and you'll never know. Her torticollis and tendency to stay on her back caused some plagiocephaly, and we were prescribed a helmet to help even out her skull while it was still soft. The people managing this work did a poor job and prematurely halted support of the helmet due to insurance issues.

At about six months of age, Elizabeth looked healthy and huge, but she was also limp, with poor muscle tone. As the months passed by, she was late in some of her milestones, such as sitting up, crawling, and walking. She also had periods of fussiness and a few fevers now and then, as well one rash that we can remember. However, her first pediatrician

dismissed all of this. We set up physical and occupational therapy to help with Elizabeth's problems. We saw a neurologist and orthopedist, who didn't see anything wrong with her physically, but the orthopedist suspected autism. We went back to our first pediatrician, who gave us a survey to fill out to determine if Elizabeth had autism. She had done this with us twice before, and both times came out negative. Typically, autism cannot be diagnosed until the child is at least eighteen months of age. Up until that time, even if the child misses some milestones, delays can easily be dismissed as "all children are different and don't develop the same." I find it interesting that even though doctors will tend to be dismissive of these things when they happen, milestones are one of the first things you are asked about when changing to a new practice or medical professional.

I always had a weird feeling when we went to see our first pediatrician; the empty office, the doctor's often distant and guarded behavior, and the completely incompetent medical assistants just scared me. The only reason we stayed as long as we did was because of insurance limitations. Plus, my wife thought I was imagining things or being paranoid. In the end I was glad we changed, and so was my wife. We were much happier with our new pediatrician, whom we have stuck with to this day.

Lessons Learned

1. Research your doctor. Take your time. Do an online investigation, and get recommendations.
2. Trust your instincts. If something doesn't feel right, *run*.
3. Don't let your doctor push you into optional vaccinations unless you feel there is special need.
4. Get copies of your records, and pay close attention to them. We've found numerous times, as with our first doctor, that the information in the records has differed from what the doctor has told us during visits.
5. Be on the lookout for any "limpness" in your child—especially with problems sitting up or rolling over.
6. Be mindful of *any* fevers, and document them carefully.

7. Document any kind of persistent fussiness or crying. *Do not be dismissive of it!* That's all too easy to do with a small child, because babies often do cry a lot, but persistent crying means there's a problem and it should not be ignored.

8. Many children do not have obvious bad reactions to vaccines or medications. The medical community will only recognize a problem as being caused by a vaccine if it's severe and immediate after application, such as grand mal seizures or severe fevers or rashes. All too often, the symptoms are much more sinister and hard to spot. Children can have:
   a. mild yet frequent fevers
   b. myoclonic seizures that make the child appear as if he or she is "dozing off"
   c. slow but progressive weakness
   d. a lot of fussiness

   Document these things if they occur, and build a dossier so you will have a case to present if needed.

9. I don't agree with making your child sleep on his or her back *all* the time. Sleeping in different positions is probably best. Discuss with your doctor, as the dogma around "back to sleep" and similar campaigns often changes over time as our knowledge of SIDS and related conditions increases. In short, I would just let the child sleep naturally and comfortably.

10. Take note if your child has issues with touching, such as kissing his or her ears, cheeks, etc. If your child gets fussy with such touching or tends to pull away, this could be a problem sign. Extreme dislike of having his or her face wiped is another indicator.

11. One of the first autistic symptoms we often hear about is lack of eye contact. That's a problem that Elizabeth never had; she always had good eye contact, and because that was most of the information about early signs of autism that I had at the time, I took comfort in thinking that this was a good negative indicator. I was wrong. Autism is often a group of symptoms—not just one thing—and every kid is different. Look for fussiness, missing milestones, limpness, avoidance of touching, and lack of eye contact.

12. Other indicators of possible autism include:
    a. hand flapping
    b. rocking
    c. staring at lights or ceiling fans
    d. lack of pretend play
    e. problems sleeping
    f. lack of pointing at objects and limited vocabulary

Note: Just seeing these symptoms intermittently or independently may not be a problem, but if you see several of these, it could indicate autism. Be mindful that I am presenting this information only as a guide. Ultimately, you must see a developmental pediatrician for a diagnosis.

3

The Diagnosis

I can do all things through him who strengthens me.
—Philippians 4:13

As I have mentioned, our first pediatrician had us do "autism evaluations" on two separate occasions. This was a short survey regarding things that Elizabeth did or did not do, her milestones, etc. The questionnaire was short, with only about ten items, and on both occasions her score showed that she was okay. When I pulled the records several months later so we could transition to a new doctor, I found that our pediatrician had indeed mentioned autism in her records as a diagnosis, although she never shared this with us openly.

Elizabeth always had good eye contact and slept well. I had kept my eyes open for those kinds of symptoms, because they are the ones you hear about the most. However, Elizabeth's problems usually centered on feeding or play activities, where she would act out or get upset. She was also slow in achieving her milestones, particularly with sitting up, crawling, and walking. The problem is that many of these things could be explained away. Elizabeth had torticollis, which resulted in a bit of strabismus in one eye. These problems could cause her some difficulty in sitting up. As mentioned previously, a child cannot really be diagnosed with autism until at least eighteen months old, because children develop at different rates, so missing or delayed milestones are not always signs of a problem. At least, this is what our first pediatrician told us.

Our new doctor recognized immediately that Elizabeth needed a professional evaluation. Such evaluations are usually performed by a developmental pediatrician, a special doctor who focuses on evaluating children for developmental delays, autism, cerebral palsy, and similar conditions affecting a child's growth or development.

The developmental pediatrician started off by asking us several questions about Elizabeth's milestones and performance. She then sat down and performed many activities with Elizabeth, some of which Elizabeth would do, and many she would not. These consisted of following some instructions, solving some simple puzzles, completing some exercises, and playing some games. She then referred Elizabeth to have an MRI to rule out any kind of cerebral palsy or related insult to the brain. We returned for a second follow-up visit to review the results of the doctor's analysis after a couple of weeks or so. Luckily, the scans came back okay; Elizabeth's brain looked normal. This doctor used something called the CARS scale to evaluate Elizabeth, and she scored a thirty-three, which is considered mild to moderate autism. The doctor then gave us references to several resources, including special schools and public as well as private programs we could take advantage of to help Elizabeth. We had a few more follow-up visits with this pediatrician, who pretty much just gave us the same evaluation and feedback each time. Over time, it became apparent that Elizabeth's autism might be a little more severe than her initial evaluation indicated.

The prognosis for such young children can be difficult to ascertain. So much can change, and many people told us that Elizabeth might just "grow out of it," although most of our doctors didn't say that. The shock of the diagnosis itself was very difficult for both of us to take. It felt as though we had just lost our child, or at least a part of her, and we mourned her death as well as the death of all our hopes and dreams for her, for our family, and for ourselves. We mourned the pain it would cause our parents and extended family. The hope that we had for this young life felt snuffed out. A rug had been pulled out from under us— more than a rug! It felt like our hearts had been torn out. Debbie and I both mourned in our own ways, sobbing uncontrollably both separately and together. Having a child provides the strongest, most powerful love a human being can experience, but losing that child, or a part of him or her, can be the most intense, heart-wrenching pain a human can feel.

Anger and doubt quickly followed the sadness. What did we do wrong? Was it me? Was it her? What did the doctors do wrong? Was it the hospital? Was it the obstetrician? Was it the pediatrician? We had our pitchforks sharpened and torches lit and were ready to land blame on the first guilty person we could find. But we realized that was not the best expenditure of our time and energy. Elizabeth was still with us, and she needed us. We still had our child, and we focused on that. It was still early in her life, she was very young, and a lot could change. We wanted to do everything we could to give Elizabeth a fighting chance. Daddy wanted to fix it, which is what Dads do! One of the first things the developmental pediatrician told us is that ABA therapy had provided the most promising results for helping autistic children; these children typically required around forty hours a week of this therapy, which would cost into the thousands. She also explained to us that the earlier these children could get the therapy, the better the long-term results would be. ABA therapy was also, of course, not covered under insurance. Despite these odds and the battle that lay before us, we were determined to fight for our baby. Our faith was our cornerstone and our foundation, and that's where we started. We had to prepare ourselves for what lay ahead and needed all the support we could get from our church and spiritual advisors.

Lessons Learned

1. Maintain a diary of your child's progress from the moment he or she is brought home from the hospital. Make notes about every key milestone: when your child lifts his or her head, rolls over, sits up, crawls, walks, says his or her first words, etc.
2. Maintain a diary of any physical issues you notice: fevers, crankiness, calls to the doctor, and anything else, no matter how small. All of this information could become critical later.
3. Get your child's Apgar scores from the hospital before you leave.
4. Note any anomalies in the way your child plays with toys or interacts with children or other people. This can be difficult, because we tend to think that babies always do things they shouldn't, such as throw tantrums, put things in their mouths, and play inappropriately,

but you should still make note of these instances, because certain patterns may emerge that could mean autism.

5. How to react to a diagnosis:
    a. Don't blame yourself or your spouse. It's not your fault. You did not do anything wrong. You need each other now more than ever, and your child needs you!
    b. In most cases, it is not necessarily anyone else's fault.
    c. Don't harbor anger. This will only eat you up inside.
    d. Redirect your energies to helping your child.

4

Going to the Altar with Pastor Mike

One of the first things my wife and I did after the diagnosis was to seek comfort in our faith. We wanted to talk to someone and wanted to prostrate ourselves before the Lord and pray for guidance and healing. My wife and I had been members of our church for about eight years. It was a large church, with over twelve thousand members. We knew few people there, but the pastor was always on fire with great sermons and was well liked. Even though the church itself was cold, lacked closeness, and felt more like going to work than to a church service, the charisma of the senior pastor overshadowed these disadvantages, so we had always remained members.

My wife and I had been saved since we were teenagers. We had no doubt about our salvation and knew God was in our hearts. But in the Southern Baptist tradition, it is not unusual to do a "rededication" when one is going through a crisis or if for some reason a person wants to rededicate himself or herself to the Lord because it had been such a long time since being saved. So when we went up front to the altar and explained to one of the assistant pastors our intention, we were redirected to about three other pastors before we were given to "Pastor Mike," one of the many assistant pastors at the church. I was a bit taken aback that we were tossed around so much. Pastor Mike escorted us out of the sanctuary and into a small office. The first thing he said was, "I hear you are in doubt about your salvation."

We looked at each other and exclaimed that was not the case; we simply wanted to rededicate ourselves and pray because our daughter had just received a devastating diagnosis.

Pastor Mike looked at us incredulously and asked, "How is your sex life? Are you getting along okay?"

My wife and I looked at each other again. "Yes, we're fine, we are worried sick about our child, get it?"

Pastor Mike went on. "What about money? How much money do you make? Are you stressed out about finances?"

I didn't think it was any of his business how much money we made, but it wasn't an unusual question at that church. I had been asked a couple of times before. We explained that based on what we were told, therapies and treatment for Elizabeth's condition could reach stratospheric proportions, but we were not in any financial stress at the moment and the cost was not our biggest concern.

Pastor Mike completely baffled us. He seemed totally clueless about the fact that we were there because we had a sick child, and he asked question after question about sex and money, to the point that it made me sick. We left in disgust. As I walked outside, I saw a big banner advertising special classes for couples to fix what they referred to as "sexual brokenness." I then began to see things a little more clearly, as experiences in some of the Sunday school classes I had attended began to add up. In one instance, when Debbie wasn't feeling well, I had attended a men's-only class. It turned out to be a class for people with addictions. Apparently, much of this church's congregation was suffering from drug and sex addictions, which had been running rampant. The way some of the people in Sunday school flirted, and the large portion of scantily clad women and girls I often saw during service—it all began to add up. We started to realize we were in the wrong church.

During the service, I had filled out a card explaining our problem and asking for prayer. When we were visited by a group of young people a few weeks later, they had no idea why they were there and just knew that we were on their "list." I invited them in to meet my wife and daughter, but they refused. They simply mentioned their Sunday school class and left.

I truly believe that these people had the best of intentions. However, whether it was Pastor Mike or the prayer group that visited us at home, everyone seemed to be on automatic pilot. They were just going through the motions, without listening or paying attention to whom they were talking to or why they were there. I think it is possible that a church can get too big for its own good. People become numb and lose interest in others, because there are so many. Leaders of these types of churches often focus on Sunday school as a way to get around this problem, but I don't think it works beyond a certain point. I believe there is a "sweet spot" or preferable size when it comes to effective congregations. I'm not sure I know what that size is, but in this case the church was definitely too big.

5

The Witch Doctor

When your child has just received a diagnosis of autism, it is sometimes difficult to think clearly. The realization that traditional medicine has totally failed, combined with the desperate need for parents to "fix" the problem, can lead to rash decisions.

Now I'm not saying that naturopathic doctors are bad; in fact, I believe many of them do a lot of good, but finding a good one is easier said than done. In our case, we located such a doctor who had a relationship with our developmental pediatrician. What we were really looking for was a doctor who followed the DAN! (Defeat Autism Now) protocol, which we will discuss in a later chapter. We preferred to find a medical doctor who subscribed to the protocol, but those proved to be few and far between. Unfortunately, there was only one medical doctor in the city who practiced this protocol, and our primary care pediatrician did not recommend her. So we opted for the naturopathic doctor our developmental pediatrician mentioned. She just happened to be very close by.

When we arrived and met the doctor, she described many of the successes she'd had with other young patients. She had several photos on the wall with her clients, most of whom were children just like Elizabeth. We chatted for a while about autism and the naturopathic approach. Elizabeth began to get fidgety, and we knew that she was about to get cranky if conditions didn't change. Back at that time, she did not like to stay still for long and would tantrum. The doctor asked a few questions and then said it was time to perform an analysis. She pulled out an electronic device called an "avatar," which had electrodes on it. These electrodes were to be connected to Elizabeth, and then a reading could be obtained. The device was some sort of computerized electrodermal screening tool based on biofeedback health technology. It was connected to a personal computer with special software and was essentially an ohmmeter, based on the work of Dr. Reinholt Voll in the 1940s. For those who do not know, an ohmmeter measures electrical impedance. Measuring this electrical impedance in various parts of the body could purportedly be meaningful. According to the doctor this reading was of the utmost importance. In fact, it seemed to be the basis for determining her recommendations. I was apprehensive at first but so desperate for answers that I was willing to try just about anything.

Elizabeth was less than cooperative, though. She began to squirm and cry and would not tolerate any kind of electrode being pinned on her. My wife tried holding her during the process, which didn't help, and the more she struggled the more upset Elizabeth became. The doctor then instructed me to put Elizabeth in my lap and try holding her while the electrodes were put on. This didn't work either. Elizabeth became even more upset. At this point the doctor asked my wife to leave the room, thinking that having fewer people in the room would decrease Elizabeth's stress level. It seemed that the doctor was somewhat annoyed at her presence, and Debbie later told me that she didn't appreciate being bossed around. It then occurred to me as I watched the doctor float about the room and chat with me that she looked very much like a witch. She had a mysterious quality about her.

We tried several times to get the electrodes attached to Elizabeth, but she simply would not tolerate it. The doctor then asked me to take my shoes off and have the electrodes connected to my feet while holding Elizabeth in my arms. This was supposed to allow Elizabeth's "life energy" to flow from her, through me, and into the avatar device so that it could be measured and analyzed. I began to seriously doubt the validity of this whole exercise. In any case, the doctor did manage to get a reading, briefly discussed the results, and came up with recommendations. She made it sound like Elizabeth needed everything, and she sold us about $800 worth of nutritional supplements and potions, all of which I quickly bought and paid for due to my inability to think clearly at the time. We took the supplements home, shoved them in the closet, and never gave Elizabeth a drop. We never returned to this doctor, who was obviously a crock. I regretted buying the supplements, but at the time I was just happy to get out of there. She'd begun to really creep me out.

Despite this experience, we didn't give up on the DAN! protocol. After some diligent searching, we found a medical doctor out of state who fit the bill.

Lessons Learned

1. Take some time to reflect and research after the initial diagnosis before doing anything else. Give it time to sink in.
2. Naturopathic doctors vary widely, and requirements to become one are different from state to state. Research them carefully.
3. Alternative medicine generally consists of three common approaches: naturopathic, integrative, and functional. I prefer functional practitioners who are also medical doctors, but do your own research, and try to get some referrals from people you trust.

6

Vaccinations

Let me say that vaccinations are one of the miracles of modern medicine. Many diseases that used to plague humankind are now virtually extinct thanks to vaccination. But just like all good things, vaccinations can be abused and overused. You don't have to be a doctor to figure that out.

When I was a child, I only had about five shots: the standard MMR (measles, mumps, and rubella) vaccine, a vaccination against polio, and perhaps one or two others. I was a child of the 1970s, and back then most people had never even heard of autism. Those shots are tried and true, and according to available data, the rise or "epidemic" of autism did not start until after 1990. I was shocked to learn that after 1990, the number of shots given to a small babe went up to about thirty different vaccinations, many applied to newborns who still had undeveloped blood-to-brain barriers. An infant is not only growing but is also still developing, much like in the womb. It just does not make sense to me to pump so many vaccinations into a small, delicate body so quickly, especially when many such diseases like hepatitis B or hepatitis C have little chance of infecting a small child. Why not wait until children are older? I wasn't vaccinated against that stuff, and I'm just fine.

I do reject the idea that autism is caused by mercury in the MMR vaccine. I believe this is a purposeful misdirection meant to discredit the entire idea of vaccinations. The MMR vaccine has been around for decades. It's tried and true; if any vaccine is causing or contributing to autism, it is not this one. More than likely, the cause is one of the thirty other odd additional shots that have been added since 1990. This is when the vaccination court was created to protect drug companies from being sued for the possible effects of vaccinations. Refer to the National Childhood Vaccine Injury Act of 1986 for more information.

I also reject the idea that the rise in autism diagnoses is due to the change in the *DSM-IV* criteria used to evaluate it. (*DSM* stands for *Diagnostic and Statistical Manual of Mental Disorders*; the *DSM-V* is now available.) One mitochondrial specialist we consulted believed this and stated that thirty years ago, our daughter would simply have been classified as "mentally retarded" instead of "autistic" because the name and criteria have changed. This does not jive with what I have seen my entire life. I went to school during the 1970s and 80s. I remember seeing the special-needs students. At every school I attended (we moved frequently when I was young, living in several states), there was generally only one class for special-needs students, and it was typically small, with children who were severely handicapped both physically and mentally. I almost never saw what would be classified as an autistic child today in such a class, a child who appears physically typical but has behavioral and communication problems. Today, most schools have entire classes dedicated to autistic children—children who have something wrong with their brains but are otherwise as normal as the other children in the school. No, my friends, it's not just the evaluation criteria that have changed. If what the doctor says is true, then back in the day, those special-needs classes would have been much larger and filled with typical-looking children with autistic traits, and I don't remember seeing any of that at all—certainly not in the volumes that we see today. Not to mention the great numbers of children we see today with allergies and learning disabilities that perhaps are not severe enough to put them on the autistic spectrum but may have also been the result of vaccinations or drug interactions when they were younger.

Yes, thousands of children are vaccinated every day with no ill effects, but I often wonder if there are hidden problems that we just cannot see. Learning disabilities, ADD, problems at school, drug addiction, or children who may not turn out as smart as they would have been are all possibilities. We could speculate all day. The truth is that some children have a predisposition for these problems. There is a genetic component.

But there's no way to tell until it happens. Mitochondrial disease is one such case, discussed in a later chapter. You may know someone with "mito" who doesn't even know he or she has it. If you are never exposed to a "trigger" or "insult" that kicks off the condition, you may go through life oblivious of it.

In Elizabeth's case, I believe it was likely the antibiotic she was given in the hospital that triggered the condition. But I can't be sure. I will never know for certain, but a parent's gut is hard to fool.

Here's my advice to parents with regards to vaccinations:

1. Have your child vaccinated.
2. But when you have your child vaccinated, be mindful of your family history. Make note of anyone who has autistic symptoms, mitochondrial disease, or related conditions. These could put you at risk.
3. Be careful of allowing any optional vaccinations or other shots that are given based on "best practice" as opposed to direct need.
4. Suggest an augmented vaccination schedule that allows for some of the shots to be given later.
5. Monitor your child *very closely* once vaccinations or other drugs are given. Bad reactions are not always obvious in infants who probably already cry a lot. Fevers and crying may also often be dismissed. Pay close attention, and look for stress, myoclonic seizures, or other unusual signs.
6. Watch doctors and nurses very closely when vaccinations are applied. Ask questions about how often these are given, how much, why, and what adverse reactions to look for.
7. When your child is a newborn in the hospital, this is when you and your child are most vulnerable. This is also when mistakes are made. Keep an eye on your child. Ask questions about how he or she is doing, and keep your child with you as much as you can. Get relatives involved to help. Make sure they understand that the world has changed and that their help is needed now.

7

Therapists

Our First ABA Therapy

There are several different types of therapy that will benefit your autistic child. They include occupational therapy, physical therapy, speech therapy, music therapy, and ABA (applied behavior analysis) therapy. Once your child is diagnosed with autism, one of the first things you will often hear is that your child needs at least forty hours per week of ABA therapy, and if you can manage to get this much therapy, there's a good chance your child will get better. This type of therapy is extremely expensive and rarely covered under insurance. Only the very wealthy can afford forty hours per week, and just about the only people who can get full coverage are those who are full-time military personnel. State laws are changing, however, and it may not be long before ABA is mandated to be covered for autistic children in most states. Even without such mandates, I've managed to get coverage through multiple appeals, but it takes a lot of work and dedication. Most insurance companies are betting that you won't have the time or energy to constantly pursue the appeals process, so each time you file, the company will automatically deny a couple of times. I eventually ended up appealing to the state to force my insurance to cover ours, but that is another story. Let me begin by describing the various therapies generally available and the programs that offer them.

The first therapist we visited after the diagnosis was an independent ABA therapist. This was a small company managed by a PhD-level practitioner who specialized in this therapy, and he had other therapists who worked under him at his direction. We had a short consultation with him, where he met Elizabeth. We didn't know much about ABA therapy, but it all sounded very good to us at the time. All we knew was that ABA therapy was not quite mainstream but was the best therapy in terms of results. The first step was to have a master's level therapist come out to our home and do what was coined as an ABELLS (assessment of basic language and learning skills) assessment. This is basically a special assessment for ABA therapy. We then decided on how many hours per week we could do and what our goals were. All the therapy was to be performed in our home. We decided on about nine hours per week, because that was the most we could afford. It was nowhere near forty hours, but we figured a little was better than nothing. The owner of the business made it plain that they would not file an insurance claim on our behalf and that we would pay out of pocket. We had two different therapists who would come at different times, usually in the mornings, and conduct their exercises with Elizabeth. One was a master's level therapist, and her rate was higher. All work was done behind closed doors. We never got to see what was being done, but we knew Elizabeth cried and fussed a good bit. At the end of each session the therapist would write a paragraph of how she did. We continued this for several months and then ceased. We didn't see much in terms of positive results, and she was so young. We later found out through a nurse that the doctor managing this therapy house had an unusual philosophy that was basically a "tough love" approach, and many in the field disagreed with it. We remembered Elizabeth's crying during the sessions and put two and two together. We believe to this day that this was a contributor to Elizabeth's fussiness and non-compliance in later years.

Babies Can't Wait

Other common sources of therapy are the "Babies Can't Wait" programs offered by your local county or state. Most regions have them in some form. This is basically a way for your child to get low-cost or free therapy; however, it's typically limited to occupational, speech, or physical therapy. ABA is not allowed in these programs in most areas. Once we found out about the program we had someone come out to our house for an interview.

Then we had to bring our child in for an evaluation, at which time they would recommend a certain number of therapies and announce the cost, which is based on income. Although these are reduced-cost therapies and are usually performed in the home, I found the quality to be lacking. The program would select outside therapists who were not always top-tier, to say the least. In one case, we had a therapist who would nose around, ask personal questions, and then call me relentlessly when the bill was due. Our case manager seemed to care about nothing except getting her paperwork signed. Based on our experience, Babies Can't Wait programs are woefully inadequate. They don't offer enough therapy to do any good, the quality is bad, and the management of the program is even worse. It's not worth the time or energy unless you have no insurance coverage at all.

During this time, I learned a valuable lesson. The Babies Can't Wait program allowed us to obtain WIC vouchers, and we decided we would try them out. The experience was eye-opening. Each time I got ready to check out, some of the cashiers would avoid me, or I would be sent down the line to someone else. More than once, I heard rude comments from the cashiers or baggers gathering the groceries. It was so bad that once I called the manager back and complained, and although he was sympathetic, it did nothing to change the embarrassment and pain that I had to go through to use those WIC vouchers. Checking out seemed to take twice as long, because the cashier had to check that I had selected the proper items, and each voucher had to be signed. It was a miserable experience that I never want to repeat. I can't imagine what it's like for people who must rely on such things every day just to make ends meet. I have a new love and sympathy for such people. I think at least once in your life each person should experience what it's like to be poor or disadvantaged, even if it's just for a few minutes. As 1 John 3:17 says, "If anyone has material possessions and sees his brother in need but has no pity on him, how can the love of God be in him?"

Physical Therapy

Elizabeth had participated in physical therapy since infanthood. This started with therapy to help her sit up, roll over, etc. Elizabeth would stand but seemed to have trouble balancing. She hated lying on her tummy and showed no interest in crawling. We became worried that she would never walk. Our fears were unfounded though, as close to her second birthday, Elizabeth began to hop like a rabbit, and not long after her second birthday, she began to stand up and walk! Within days she was even running back and forth down the halls! We were so happy. We had prayed so much because we thought Elizabeth would never walk; her second birthday was long past the usual timing for this milestone, but every child moves at his or her own pace and God also has his own timeline. Elizabeth went from nothing to hopping and then walking in what seemed like no time at all. It felt like a miracle, and perhaps it was. But it was God's way. God has a way of making sure that certain things happen, and just because they don't happen on the "typical" timeline doesn't mean that they never will. As Proverbs 3:5–6 reads, "Trust in the Lord with all your heart, and do not lean on your own understanding. In all your ways acknowledge him, and he will make straight your paths."

Occupational and Speech Therapy

OT and ST, as they are often called, are the most common forms of therapy for any developmentally delayed child. During occupational therapy, or OT, our therapists work with sensory integration issues and everyday tasks. Many autistic children suffer from hypotonia, or muscle weakness. It was difficult for us to understand this with our child because she was as strong as an ox. However, it is not about strength; it is about coordination. Elizabeth can quickly get the best of us when it comes to horseplay, but she has difficulty putting on her clothes, buttoning buttons, or tying shoes. Tasks that require a certain level of finger dexterity can be especially difficult. Occupational therapy helps children develop the skills and dexterity to complete everyday tasks and to get over some of the sensory issues they have.

Speech therapy, or ST, focuses on exactly what the name implies. Communication issues are one of the hallmarks of autism, and such therapy is often continued for extended periods. Language ability can vary widely from child to child with autism. Children with autism range from being very talkative to being completely nonverbal. Receptive language can vary just as widely and is not necessarily linked to an inability to speak. A child who talks little or not at all may understand you very well. In Elizabeth's case, we are convinced that her receptive language is near typical, with her primary deficits being in communicating outward. She had a couple of jumps in speaking ability when she was younger, going from being almost nonverbal to being able to communicate most of her wants and needs within a short period of time. Her ability to describe objects and speak about abstract concepts is progressing very slowly and often seems to ebb and flow.

We've had a few different occupational and speech therapists over the years, mostly due to insurance-coverage issues. Progress in these therapies can be slow but is usually steady. I would encourage any parent to get his or her autistic child into a regular speech and occupational therapy program if possible and if your doctor agrees. Therapies need to be performed multiple times a week, and scheduling can be a challenge. Be flexible, and your therapists will be flexible with you. This will allow your child to get the most out of these therapies.

Feeding Problems and Therapies

Elizabeth had always been a picky eater. As a toddler, she would only eat certain things. This can be true for many typical children, and our pediatrician assured us not to be alarmed. He said kids always seem to balance themselves, even if it seems they are not eating the best. Elizabeth used to eat oatmeal, cereal, a few vegetables, and even eggs. However, over time she lost interest in these foods. In fact, it seemed as if her food preferences became even more restrictive as she got older, not less so. Eventually, she stopped eating pretty much anything except chicken nuggets and hot dogs. She drank a lot of V8 Fusion fruit juice, which we credit for her getting at least some semblance of vegetable intake. Most vitamins are in pill or gummy form, both of which she rejected.

Elizabeth had a penchant for breaking up her food into tiny little bites and slipping them into her mouth while at the same time dropping crumbs on the floor. It seemed that she was getting about as much food on the floor as she was in her mouth. We had some food therapy evaluations performed at an autism center in our city, and we had a conversation with a gastrointestinal doctor. The best conclusion we could come to was that the problem was oral sensitivity. It didn't have anything to do with her gut, as best as they could tell. This was a relief to us, because we figured the food sensitivity was something we could work with. Many children on the spectrum have severe gastrointestinal issues, which can be incredibly stressful and difficult to manage.

Elizabeth's eating patterns didn't seem to be negatively affecting her until she was about eight years old. At this time, she stopped eating oatmeal, cereal, and other grains. We also noticed that she wasn't eating at school as much, mainly because the new teacher wasn't patient with her slow eating pace. She lost a lot of weight and became alarmingly thin. At one point, she caught a stomach virus during the winter and stopped eating altogether. We had to take her to the hospital for an overnight stay. We were worried to death that she would have to have a stomach or feeding tube inserted permanently to keep her nourished. In our minds, this would have been the first step in a downward spiral. Fortunately, that didn't happen. She was able get enough nutrition in the hospital to be released, and our doctor prescribed a medication to boost her appetite. She ate well during the coming months and gained weight. However, we continued the feeding therapy on a regular basis to try to get her to eat more varied foods. There is a concept our therapist told us about called "food jagging," which occurs if a child eats too much of one food for a long period. This will cause the child to suddenly stop eating that food for anywhere from several months to a year or longer. The therapist suggested that was happening with Elizabeth and her oatmeal and cereal.

Music Therapy

One of the first therapies we started with Elizabeth when she was a baby was music therapy, and she took to it right away. It wasn't long before she started singing and even developed a very impressive vibrato! The trick was getting her to sing what and when we wanted her to. That was a bit tough. But for years, Elizabeth enjoyed her music therapy, which brought a special light into our life. Unfortunately, most of the time it is not covered under insurance and can be quite expensive, so we were not always able to keep it up. However, I highly recommend it if you can do it for your child. You never know what talents might come to the surface, and it does so much for children. Music helps keep Elizabeth calm and content. There's also nothing more fun than singing and clapping along with your child. To this day Elizabeth gets so excited when we start singing, which translates into her church life too, as she really enjoys the sing-alongs in her children's church service. The Bible celebrates music making as holy:

> Oh come, let us sing to the Lord; let us make a joyful noise to the rock of our salvation! Let us come into his presence with thanksgiving; let us make a joyful noise to him with songs of praise! (Psalm 95:1–2)

> Let the word of Christ dwell in you richly, teaching and admonishing one another in all wisdom, singing psalms and hymns and spiritual songs, with thankfulness in your hearts to God. (Colossians 3:16)

Lessons Learned

1. If your child has feeding issues, pay close attention to food jagging. Consider talking to a feeding therapist.
2. Therapies are definitely worth it. Progress can be slow or incremental, but the right therapies will pay off. Be patient, and get all the therapy you can for your child.

8

The DAN! Protocol

When Elizabeth was first diagnosed in 2009, the DAN! (Defeat Autism Now!) Protocol was a popular treatment method for autistic children. This protocol was a biomedical approach promoted by the Autism Research Institute. Although we knew it was a bit controversial and "on the edge," we were willing to try anything to help our little girl. The DAN! website had a list of doctors who had attended the DAN! seminars and practiced the protocol, but there weren't many of them. There were two practices in our state. One office never returned our calls, and our primary pediatrician did not recommend the other doctor. Although our pediatrician did not do the DAN! protocol himself, he did not dissuade us from following up on it. We finally found a practitioner in Tennessee and began seeing him. He was a medical doctor and experienced in the protocol. The protocol involves running several metabolic tests and then making recommendations for supplements. We saw our DAN! doctor periodically for a couple of years. We followed the protocol almost to completion but stopped short of performing the chelation procedures, which was the final step in the process. We just thought that would be too strenuous on Elizabeth, and the good it would do might not have been worth the pain. We noticed that Elizabeth's fussiness began to improve dramatically with the treatments that we did. I believe she was experiencing a lot of tummy pain and gut discomfort at the time, which the treatments helped with. The testing also revealed something about mitochondria. The DAN! doctor told us that Elizabeth has a specific type of mitochondrial gene that is present in a significant percentage of the population—the same population that some believe is susceptible to vaccine issues and other problems. At the time, this was just a passing comment, but it got my wheels turning about mitochondria and eventually led to Elizabeth's mito (mitochondrial disease) diagnosis. I should state for the record that research around these issues is progressing quickly and changing often.

The DAN! Protocol is now considered defunct. The Autism Research Institute no longer supports it, although you can probably still find doctors who do it. The protocol has been replaced by more behavioral approaches.

So, do I recommend the DAN! Protocol? Well, often the protocol seems to involve throwing a lot of supplements at the problem that may not have immediate benefits. But in our case, I am positive that Elizabeth was experiencing tummy or leaky gut issues that were improved by the protocol, and the information I got from all the tests was insightful, made me more educated, and led to our diagnosis of mitochondrial disease, which would not have happened without DAN!. Indeed, her mitochondrial specialist even continued a couple of the supplements.

However, parts of the protocol, such as chelation, are controversial, and DAN! is now considered somewhat out of date. There were also problems with the protocol not being uniformly applied. The Autism Research Institute merely listed practitioners who had attended its seminars, but it did not perform any kind of certification. So, the methodology used by practitioners varied widely, as we noticed ourselves when working with two such professionals. I suggest considering all alternatives and considering what is best for your child. Follow your instincts. They usually won't lead you astray. Mine didn't.

Lessons Learned

1. With autism, so little is known and so little help is available that nothing is wrong with exploring alternative treatments. Do your research, pray for guidance, and you will find what works best for your child.

2. As with any professional, do your research and get recommendations. Most people are working hard to help families suffering from autism, but there are those who will take advantage of you.
3. Be wary of articles, resources, or people that totally deride one approach or another. There are too many variables and few absolutes in this situation.

9

Insurance Headaches

Insurance coverage can be a big issue for parents of autistic children. Autism is often classified as a mental condition rather than a physical or medical one and may fall under different parts of your policy. Additionally, many services that these children desperately need, such as ABA therapy, are minimally covered or not covered at all. Even traditionally covered therapies, such as occupational, physical, or speech therapy, may be limited to a certain number of sessions per year. This is because insurance is largely designed to get you through temporary illnesses or conditions—not ongoing issues like autism.

Most autistic children will need all or some combination of the therapies previously mentioned. My suggestion is to get prescriptions for these therapies from your primary care physician and engage a local, well-recommended provider as soon as possible. Most providers will help you with insurance filings and checking on coverage. If they don't, look elsewhere. If a provider is not willing to help you get them paid, then they don't think much of their patients, which will translate into service issues as well. Good, caring providers are out there. The next thing you can do is sign up for a Babies Can't Wait program, which is likely offered by your county or local government. Virtually all counties in the United States have these programs or something similar. As mentioned previously, it will not be enough therapy on its own, but it will get your child therapy at a discounted rate or perhaps even for free, and combined with other therapies, it will help give your child the support he or she needs. Signing up for these programs usually involves a short interview, followed by an evaluation of your child by specialists. Program staff will then come up with recommendations for therapy and quote you any associated costs. Babies Can't Wait programs are typically only available for very young children, usually under three years of age. But as most experts will tell you, the earlier you can begin therapy for autistic children, the better.

The next thing you need to do is apply for any Medicaid programs available in your state. These are commonly referred to as "deeming waivers" or "Katy Beckett" programs. These programs can be invaluable in supplementing the insurance coverage you already have. For example, if your insurance only covers twenty speech therapy sessions per year, then the Medicaid waiver can pick up the slack so that you can have sessions all year long, every week. Getting these waivers can be rather difficult. There is a lot of red tape and a lot of required documentation that the application does not always tell you about. We applied twice on our own and were turned down until we finally hired a specialist to help us. I highly recommend that you locate someone in your area who helps parents apply for these programs. It won't be cheap, but it will be worth it in the end. Once you get the waiver, it will need to be renewed each year; sometimes renewal requires a full application, and other times it only requires a short update. Typically, these programs require a psychological evaluation, summaries, and notes from all therapists your child sees; a signed letter and completed application form from the child's pediatrician; any hospital records; updated medical records; and more. It's a difficult process to wade through for any parent, especially if you are unfamiliar with it.

The trickiest service to get insurance coverage for is ABA therapy. If you are active military, your family will probably have pretty good coverage for this. Otherwise, it will likely be difficult. If you have it, consider yourself lucky. The laws in each state are slowly but surely changing to require insurance companies to provide support for this kind of therapy. If your insurance company turns you down, push the appeals process as hard as you can. After many appeals, we finally got coverage for a huge ABA therapy bill once we escalated it to the state level; this was before a new law in our state was passed demanding coverage for children six and under. Our provider was flabbergasted that we managed to get it covered. It takes persistence and a lot of energy, which can be in limited supply when you are managing the needs of your child along with everything else you must do, but in our case, we were particularly motivated by a large bill. We then changed providers to someone who had no trouble at all getting the therapy covered by our insurance. What a difference a good provider can make! Of course, these kinds of providers are hard to get appointments with and are usually booked up because everyone knows they can get coverage. The mediocre providers who don't help with insurance always have tons of openings. We had to be very persistent about getting our daughter admitted to a provider who could cover us. An example of a good appeal letter can be found below.

Example of Appeal Letter for ABA Therapy Coverage

September 10, 2010

Department of Community Health
Division of Health Planning

Carrier: Company A
Re: Your Child
ID: 000000
Dates of Service: November 12, 2009,
                   through April 29, 2010

To whom it may concern:

I am writing to request a review of Company A's determination to deny outpatient therapy services to my daughter. The denial I received from X indicates "Applied Behavioral Analysis therapy is not a covered benefit under the member's mental health benefit plan. Applied Behavioral Analysis is considered an unproven or experimental service, and the member's plan does not cover unproven or experimental services."

My insurance plan allows twenty outpatient behavioral health visits per year. According to state law, my child cannot be precluded from receiving these services due to her autism diagnosis. Company A is perpetuating a misapplication of benefits because of her diagnosis and is avoiding issuing payment of her claims. They will not specifically state that they consider the services "not medically necessary"; rather, Company A states they are unproven, which is essentially stating the same thing. Unproven services are not considered eligible, because they are exactly that: unproven or not accepted as the "standard of care" and therefore not of any benefit to my child. *This is untrue.*

The therapy my child is receiving is medically necessary and *proven* effective in treating children with autism. I have included the American Academy of Pediatrics report entitled "Management of Children with Autism Spectrum Disorders," which supports the use of a multifaceted approach in treatment. Applied Behavioral Analysis is listed as a medically necessary and appropriate treatment.

I am requesting that my case be reviewed and coverage provided in accordance with my outpatient behavioral health benefit. I appreciate your review in this matter.

Sincerely,

Another insurance headache is supplements. If you are giving your child CoQ10, carnitine, B12 shots, or any kind of treatment that is considered a vitamin supplement, getting coverage will be difficult, if not impossible. Some of these highly concentrated supplements can be very expensive. In our case, we had to bite the bullet on this for a while, but in the end we cancelled the supplements because we could not see much long-term difference. We believe they helped early on, but as our daughter grew, her food allergies and gut problems largely subsided. Some supplements are still recommended, but our doctor does not place great emphasis on them, and when we do administer them, it's difficult to tell if they make a difference. As I will emphasize throughout this book, every case is different, and yours may be as well. I would encourage you to explore all options to find what works best for your child.

Lessons Learned

1. Know your coverage: Check your insurance for current coverage levels on ABA, OT, PT, speech, and even music therapies. Learn and know your coverage well. You will need to be an expert on it. Learn the appeals process well too.
2. Locate good therapists who will help with insurance filings. If they won't help, keep looking.
3. If your child is under three years of age, sign up for a Babies Can't Wait program to supplement your insurance.
4. Deeming waiver/Medicaid: Apply for your state's Medicaid or deeming waiver program. Get help if you need it. Check with local Facebook groups, your doctor, and your therapists for recommendations on hiring someone to help.

10

The Neurologist

We had briefly seen a neurologist who was part of a larger pediatric neurology practice. He did not see any problems with Elizabeth, but he did recommend a scan to rule anything out. The doctor was great, but he was tied to a large practice with staff who routinely fouled up insurance filings, prescriptions, and orders for the scan. We decided to find an independent doctor, hoping that a smaller practice would provide better service.

Our second neurologist seemed to have a good bedside manner and, in the beginning, was attentive and astute about making recommendations and following up. We completed the scan, which showed no problems or abnormalities with Elizabeth's brain. He completed some blood work, which included a metabolic workup. This did not reveal anything significant either, apart from an anomaly related to mitochondrial function. At the time, the doctor did not think this was significant. However, I had remembered something similar from the testing performed by our DAN! doctor, and I voiced my concern. The neurologist then referred us to a couple of mitochondrial specialists. We were lucky in that two such experts were available in our area. This is the kind of expertise that many people end up flying all over the world for, and we could get face-to-face meetings with these doctors right in our backyard.

Our neurologist emphasized his belief that Elizabeth did not have any kind of mitochondrial disease. Of course, he did the typical tests for everything else, such as fragile X and Rhett's syndrome, both of which we were pretty sure Elizabeth didn't have based on the amniocentesis that had been done and the fact that they are typically very severe in presentation. As we discuss in a later chapter, our neurologist turned out to be incorrect. We continued to see him periodically for follow-ups, and one thing that we noticed is that he basically didn't do anything but ask us questions, make notes, and then get up to leave after about three minutes. Each visit was unproductive. To our aggravation, he would repeatedly ask us the same questions: Has Elizabeth always been delayed? Has Elizabeth always had autism? He would then ask us more questions about her previous milestones. All of this seemed a bit irrelevant because it was in the past, and we couldn't see how this would relate to any kind of treatment. Further, we weren't developmental pediatricians and did not consider ourselves experts in determining how long she had been delayed, when she came down with autism, and so on. As we had been told previously, children often develop at different rates. It's difficult to determine if any delay is really a delay at all, or whether it even matters, at least until the child is eighteen to twenty months old.

To our chagrin, we found out later that the doctor was documenting this in Elizabeth's medical records. When it came time for us to request a copy of these records, we had a hard time getting them. The staff goldbricked us and asked us repeatedly about why we needed them. When we got the records and read them, we were shocked. Much of what was in there the doctor had not discussed with us. One thing he had highlighted in his notes was "parents said that child has always been delayed." This statement was a twisted account of what we had originally said; we had explained that we weren't qualified to say whether our child had developmental delays or not. Such notes caused us problems later when we sought the help Elizabeth needed.

We stopped seeing this neurologist.

Lessons Learned

1. Regularly request copies of your medical records, preferably after each visit. Ask for full disclosure, and tell your doctor it's for personal reasons. You have a legal right to those records.
2. When a doctor asks about our children's development, we always want to try to give good answers. We want to be good parents.

The problem is, the real answer is that we don't know for sure and probably aren't qualified to provide any kind of developmental evaluation. When a doctor asks you about your child's development, unless you are absolutely sure, tell him or her that you "don't know." That's really the best answer because if you aren't sure, you really don't know. Feeling under pressure to give an accurate answer when you aren't sure about it could come back to bite you. The doctor will note your answer, and it will become a permanent part of your child's medical records. It will cause you headaches later. If you aren't absolutely sure about dates your child achieved certain milestones or when specific behaviors started, don't guess.

3. Ask for copies of any scans or MRIs. Be sure to get the scans on a CD in electronic format, not just the doctor's notes.

4. It makes no difference whether you go to an independent doctor or a large practice. The staff in both situations can be just as sorry. Honestly, a smaller practice doctor is often a lower performer unless he or she is well renowned, which leads to my next recommendation.

5. Get references for any new doctor. A lot of them. Get tied into Facebook or groups in your area that talk about autism or children with special needs. Other parents will give you good recommendations.

6. Raise your concerns, and go with your gut. Press your doctor for resolution. If I had not pursued the mitochondrial aspect based on my gut instinct, we would never had gotten Elizabeth a proper diagnosis.

11

The Lawsuit

The issues I encountered during Elizabeth's birth and during her treatment by her first pediatrician continued to gnaw at me. I began to do my own research regarding autism, its potential causes, and the positions of the medical community on the topic. Like many parents, I wanted to accept what my doctors told me, that autism is a largely inherited condition that isn't anyone's fault. But also like many parents, my instincts told me otherwise. No one in my family or my wife's family had been affected by any kind of autism spectrum issue. Even when looking at extended relatives, there wasn't any history at all.

Doctors try to explain away these issues by stating that the *DSM-IV* criteria and the way these children are evaluated and diagnosed have changed over the years. They also state that there is no research proving that vaccines or other drugs cause autism. However, just because there's no research proving something does not mean the problem isn't there. Many of these conditions lack thorough research. Research takes years to conduct and even longer to get published. It also requires funding, much of which comes from pharmaceutical companies.

I read about the case of Hannah Poling, who received the first court award in a vaccine-autism claim. Many of her symptoms were similar to what our child experienced: fevers, refusal to eat, tantrums, and other traits characteristic of autism. The award in the case was significant, amounting to about $20 million over the child's lifetime. Her father was a medical doctor, so to some degree, her family had access that most people do not.

I decided to explore legal options. I began by contacting local attorneys, most of whom did not know where to start. I did get a little useful input from one firm, which told me that these kinds of issues had to be handled through a special court, called vaccine court, and that you had only three years to file. Thus began the saga.

I contacted attorneys who, in turn, referred me to other attorneys. I eventually got in contact with three different lawyers who'd had previous successes in such cases. However, I was taken aback at the response I got. One attorney, without even knowing any facts of the case, responded with something to the effect of, "Your case will go nowhere."

How could this guy say this without knowing any of the facts? I was not an attorney, but I had attended law school, and even I knew that you had to know the facts of a case to make sense of it. It was such a strange reaction. After a lot of rigmarole and pressing many of these attorneys for answers, I discovered the following:

1. It's about the money: one attorney confided that he didn't want to do one of these cases again because they took forever, and the vaccine court was slow to pay.
2. Rules: a couple of lawyers told me that I would not have a case, and they would not accept a case, unless it met one of the following two criteria:
   a. The child had documented seizures following the application of a vaccine or drug.
   b. The child's mitochondrial disease diagnosis had been proven by muscle biopsy.

I was led to believe that if we didn't meet one of these criteria, I wouldn't have a chance. Since I knew Elizabeth had not had any severe, documented seizures, I set about the mitochondrial disease route. As I have alluded to earlier, I suspected that Elizabeth had this condition, but it was only a hunch.

We spent over a year getting the diagnosis, a process I discuss in the next chapter. The mistake I made was that I lost an entire year by waiting. I should have gone ahead and made a filing with the court and then proceeded with the diagnosis.

Finally, with the diagnosis in hand, I approached a few of the attorneys I had contacted before. I thought I had a slam dunk this time, but boy, was I surprised. Those attorneys had the same reaction as before. Despite my documentation, no one wanted to take the case. There was no money in it for them. And some of these lawyers had nasty reactions. I contacted law firms from all over the country. Anyone I knew who had even a little experience with these types of cases got a call from me. The website for the vaccine court had a list of attorneys who were supposedly experienced and willing to take such cases. This was of no use to me at all. The ones located in my state did not even return my calls. I was bordering on despair when I finally found one local attorney who was willing to take the case. He even brought in two other attorneys who could assist! I was elated. The lawyer in question also had a child with special needs. I thought to myself, *This person understands.* All three of them came to our house, and we had a long discussion. Much of the talk revolved around outlining each person's role and skills. The next step was to provide all the available medical records so that we could do the initial filing.

After spending quite some time gathering all the records I could, I turned them over to the attorney's office. A few days went by, and then suddenly, without explanation, I got a call telling me that they would not be taking the case. I was flabbergasted. They did not explain why. One of the junior attorneys dropped by to turn over the records, which were now compiled into a nice, organized folder. I could get a few facts out of her but not the entire explanation. However, when reviewing the records myself (which I had not done up until this time), I found a few surprises.

1. Our first pediatrician noted in her records a suspicion of autism that she had not conveyed to us. We'd raised the concern and she'd had us do a couple of tests, as I have explained previously, but she always explained it away and said that Elizabeth was doing fine.
2. Our neurologist, as I've mentioned, stated in the records, "Parents said that the child has always been delayed." This is not true. Elizabeth had normal Apgar scores and was lifting her head the day she was born!

3. These two issues made it appear as though Elizabeth had come down with autism much earlier than what we believed. This put us outside the three-year filing limitation. I thought that since children cannot be officially diagnosed with autism until they are at least eighteen months old anyway, we were in the clear. But our attorneys did not have the stomach to fight that.

I was devastated. After so much work, we were getting nowhere, and the deadline to file was running out. Elizabeth was formally diagnosed at around a year and a half, and I'd been using that as our starting point for the three-year clock. Although my attorneys thought I had no chance, I knew that if I didn't file by that deadline I would certainly be out of luck. My next step was to file "pro se," which is a way parents can file on their own, without an attorney. This can be done via a website or through the mail. Since websites are always changing, I have not included the web address here, but it can be found easily via a web search.

I believe that the three-year limitation is wrong. It's not long enough. Diagnosis often takes years, and determining autism early is difficult. But the law says three years from the first signs of symptoms, whether you have a diagnosis or not. When the science doesn't support diagnosing at such a young age, and you have a doctor who tells you children develop at different speeds and not to be concerned, having a case is very difficult. How can you take on the expense and trouble of a court case without a thorough diagnosis? How can you litigate such a case until you are sure that there is a problem? How can you find a doctor who will serve as an expert witness without such a diagnosis? The problem is that the vaccine court is designed to support cases where there is a severe, immediate, and obvious insult. If your child wasn't writhing in pain and convulsing wildly on the floor after a shot, you don't have a case. Even the mitochondrial route is very difficult without obvious trauma. The hard truth, in my opinion, is that autism and mitochondrial disease symptoms can be very subtle until a certain age, and by then, the legal clock has often run out. Little babies can have fevers and myoclonic seizures that are easily dismissed by parents and doctors alike until it is too late.

At first, the idea of representing myself seemed daunting and bordered on hopeless. However, since I had been to law school, I thought I owed it to myself and my family to at least try. In reality, the filing and court process was not that bad. Putting together the initial materials was the worst part, which my previous attorney had helped me with. I had to put them on CD and ship multiple copies to the Department of Health and Human Services in addition to the court. This got quite expensive, especially since I was sending it near the deadline. You should know that although there are a lot of ways to file things online, there is a limitation for parents filing pro se. Attorneys can do pretty much everything electronically, but pro se applicants must do most filings via mail or FedEx.

Vaccine courts do not have judges; instead they have something called "Special Masters," which, for all intents and purposes, is the same thing. I also noted that the attorney assigned to our case for the Department of Health and Human Services was young and relatively inexperienced, although she had a group of experienced people advising her.

Once you submit the initial filing, the court or defense will often ask for additional records or documents. You will need to file these as they are requested. You will also need to file status reports from time to time. I was pleasantly surprised to find that the court clerk was available, helpful, and sympathetic to parents. I had no trouble getting the information I needed. Online resources are not bad either. The attorneys I talked to did not agree. My guess is that court officials are less lenient with them. I remember the clerk asking me in a stern voice if I was an attorney, and when I told him I was a parent filing pro se, his attitude changed.

Below is an example of a status report for the court. Note the distance I go to in describing the status of each item the court requested.

Example of a Status Report

US Court of Federal Claims
Washington, DC 20005
RE: Anon v. HHS, No. 00000
Status Report for Medical Filing and Request for Extension

Dr. David A. Bishop

Dear Special Master and Opposing Attorney:

I am writing to request a thirty-day extension of my filing deadline for the medical records as discussed on December 5, 2014. Below is a status report of all items requested, as required in the order filed December 6, 2014:

1. **Contemporaneous medical records in support of paragraph 4 of the petition:** I have these in my possession. I am currently compiling them in the format required by the court.

2. **Complete updated records from Dr. M:** I have these in my possession. I am currently compiling them in the format required by the court.

3. **Complete Records from Dr. N:** This office has been largely unavailable during the holiday, but I now a request filed. I expect to have these very soon and compiled as required.

4. **Complete records from therapists:** These were already submitted as exhibit 7 in the initial filing. Just to be sure, I want to double-check once more before filing my "statement of completion."

5. **Complete records from Dr. B:** This office was closed during the holiday, but I have placed a request for these records and am waiting on a response.

6. **Complete and updated records from Developmental Pediatrics:** The initial evaluation (which includes the diagnosis of autism) and the latest evaluation from 2012 are included as exhibits 2 and 3, respectively, in the filing. The only items missing are annual evaluations from 2010 and 2011, which I have requested from the doctor. The office has been unavailable during the holidays.

I greatly appreciate your patience in this matter. The holiday season in December and early January has made it more difficult to obtain and compile these items before the deadline (due to doctor's office closures and my own work schedule). I also take the "statement of completion" very seriously and am adamant about making sure I have absolutely everything submitted that has been requested, so I am checking it twice. However, I am confident that I will have everything filed by the next deadline. As required by the court, I have contacted the opposing attorney, and she has agreed to the extension without opposition. I have also filed the certificate of service as required (see attached).

Thank you,

Always be respectful, responsive, and complete when replying to the court's requests. Once I obtained all the records that were asked for, I provided the final filing. An example of such a filing is below:

Example of Completed Filing

February 20, 2014

US Court of Federal Claims
Washington, DC 20005
RE: Anon v. HHS, No. 00000
Medical Filing

Dear Special Master and Opposing Attorney:

I am writing to complete our submission of medical records for our daughter. Below is an outline describing each new exhibit. The compact disc with each of the new records is enclosed (including the required copies). Also, please find enclosed our statement of completion and certificate(s) of service.

Ex.	Description	Pages
14	Dr. B: Complete records	1–9
15	Dr. G: 2010 annual evaluation	1–3
16	Dr. G: 2011 annual evaluation	1–3
17	Dr. N: Complete records	1–22
18	Dr. M: Summary letter, July 1, 2012	1–7
19	Dr. M: Follow-up report from July 21, 2012	1–18
20	Dr. M: Follow-up report from November 24, 2012	1–8
21	Dr. M Follow-up report November 6, 2012	1–18
22	Dr. M: JCN article on mitochondrial disease and developmental regression	1–4
23	Dr. M: JCN article linking fever to mitochondrial disease and regression	1–7
24	Therapists: Physical therapy evaluations for 2009 and 2010	1–8
25	Therapists: Speech therapy initial evaluation 2009	1–8

Additional Explanations

Also, as per the court's requirement, I am submitting the following explanations detailing why some records requested are not available:

Occupational Therapy

After detailed review with the OT, it appears that no annual assessment was performed in 2010. All that exists are the initial evaluation in 2009 and a final one in 2011. Our insurance only pays for twenty visits per year, after which time we would cease occupational therapy until the following year. If not enough time had passed since the last evaluation, then one was not performed.

Additional Records of Fever Episodes in Support of Paragraph 4 of the Petition

Fevers were usually not handled with office visits. If Elizabeth experienced them, we would contact a nurse at the pediatrician's office for guidance, who would simply inform us to hydrate her and use fever reducer. These calls may not have been logged. In time, the nurse informed us that it was no longer necessary to contact the office regarding these episodes, as they were not deemed serious. We were informed that "fevers are no longer considered as serious as they once were" with children. As a result, we stopped calling these events in and treated them as previously instructed. Tragically, we now know this was the wrong approach with our daughter. Although experiencing a fever after administration of a vaccine is not a serious issue with a typical child (and often a common occurrence), with children affected by mitochondrial disease it is extremely serious. Elizabeth's doctors and her school teachers are now instructed to send Elizabeth immediately to the emergency room at the local children's hospital if she presents with fever. Failure to do so can result in the symptoms as stated in Paragraph 4 of the petition, which are supported by Dr. B's assessment just a few weeks after our daughter's most recent inoculation. See also Dr. M's papers and reports regarding fevers and regression as related to mitochondrial disease.

Like many parents, we are subject to the available science and current knowledge of our practitioners. Fortunately, this knowledge is changing at a rapid pace for the better. Unfortunately, it came too late for our daughter.

Thank you,

Sympathy works. Don't be afraid to explain to the court the difficulties of your current situation and what you are going through to obtain the records needed. Just be honest. I found the court to be understanding and professional—much more so than the insurance companies I appealed to in the past.

At some point, the court will be satisfied with the records received and will issue a response. This response will likely require you to submit an expert report. This means that you need to find a doctor with the proper expertise to write a report on your behalf. This can be difficult, because there are few doctors with the necessary expertise and even fewer who are willing to consider supporting a vaccination case. These doctors are also very busy, and their time is expensive. Yes, that's right. Even though you may have insurance coverage that takes care of office visits and treatments, these doctors charge big bucks to support litigation. We were shocked at the four-figure fee our doctor wanted to merely write the report. Fees for physically attending court and testifying were even more shocking. Due to all of these factors, getting the report took more time than we thought, and a time extension request became necessary. Below is an example of such a request.

Example of Extension Request for Filing Expert Report

US Court of Federal Claims
Washington, DC 20005
RE: Anon v. HHS, No. 00000
Request for Extension for Filing Expert Report

Dear Special Master and Opposing Attorney:

I am writing to request a ninety-day extension of my filing deadline for the Expert Report that was requested on March 3, 2013.

Our original appointment with our expert was scheduled in June but was rescheduled to late July due to a scheduling error by the doctor's office personnel. We've also discovered that it will now take several weeks for the expert to review the records completely and write the report.

As you know, experts in this field are very few and in high demand. As a result, scheduling appointments and receiving responses seem to take much longer.

I greatly appreciate your patience in this matter.

As required by the court, I have contacted the opposing attorney, and she has agreed to the extension without opposition. I have also filed the certificate of service as required (see attached).

Thank you,

Eventually our doctor got around to reviewing our case and refused to take it on. She said that we would have a difficult time due to some of the things that were placed into the records. Basically, these were the same reasons our lawyers had refused to help. Fortunately, she was nice enough to point the issues out to us. Many of the records were illegible and confusing. I responded to our doctor accordingly, thanking her for her time but also providing explanations for the anomalies in the records. We needed to work with this doctor in an ongoing basis and wanted to preserve the relationship.

Dr. K,

Thank you for your review. We only recently noticed the items you called out when we pulled Elizabeth's records for this case. We were distressed and shocked at the items that some of the physicians and therapists had placed in her records, because we did not feel they were accurate and, furthermore, they were never discussed with us.

For example, although Elizabeth had been a little behind in a couple of her milestones, Dr. D always told us that "children develop at different rates" and that nothing could be diagnosed until she was eighteen months of age. She took a "wait and see" approach. We always had good smiling, eye contact, babbling, etc. She was only slow at some gross motor issues, so we never really suspected anything. She was referred to Dr. B, who told us he didn't see any problems except the slight hypotonia. Obviously, his record says different. At no time were we told that Elizabeth was being documented as "developmentally delayed," nor were the ramifications of that "diagnosis" discussed with us. Dr. D administered "autism tests" during our last two visits with her, both of which were negative. This test was based on a questionnaire that Dr. D had us fill out during the appointment. This testing is mysteriously absent from her records. At one of Elizabeth's appointments in her first year, there was confusion in Dr. D's office. When the MA came in to give Elizabeth her shots, the shot she said she was administering was different from what the doctor had told us just a moment before. An argument ensued outside the room, and the MA was terminated. We never got any answers about what happened. We later left Dr. D when we discovered several complaints about her online.

There are few records of Elizabeth's fevers because every time we called the pediatric office, they would tell us not to worry about it. In fact, they eventually told us that we no longer needed to call them about Elizabeth's fevers because "fevers are no longer considered a serious issue in toddlers." We were told just to give her pain reliever until they subsided, which they usually did. We now know, based on Dr. M's research, that fevers can have serious impacts on regression, a fact that neither we nor any of her practitioners were aware of at the time.

We certainly never told any of her doctors that she had "always been developmentally delayed." In fact, we always wanted it understood that we were not medical doctors and were unaware of the clinical definition of "developmental delay" or what the ramifications could be for a court case. We know now, thanks to you.

On one hand, we are deeply disappointed with the people who have worked with Elizabeth. On the other hand, we have a better understanding of what is going on. We just wish her practitioners had spent as much time helping her and communicating with *us* as they did documenting behind her to cover themselves.

Thanks so much for your time and help. On a lighter note, we have completed the swallow study and blood work you recommended. You should have already received the results. As we turn our focus to helping our daughter and her condition, we look forward to continuing to work with you.

Without a doctor's support, your case is essentially dead in the water. Even if our doctor had agreed, the cost overruns would have been enormous—although plaintiffs are eventually recompensed for those in the end. We were stuck with nowhere to go, no alternatives. Eventually we had to provide a status report with an explanation. An example of such a report can be found below.

Example of Status Report for Dismissal

US Court of Federal Claims
Washington, DC 20005
RE: Anon v. HHS, No. 00000
Status Report

Dear Special Master and Opposing Attorney:

Per the order received on November 8, I am providing the following status report.

After receiving the order on May 3 to provide an expert report, we consulted our medical team, specifically Elizabeth's neurologist, Dr. N. Dr. N stated that providing an expert opinion regarding vaccinations and mitochondrial disease was outside of his realm of expertise and referred us to Dr. K. Dr. K is widely recognized as an expert in this area and handles many similar cases. Dr. K's services are in high demand, and appointments had to be scheduled far in advance. However, we managed to secure an appointment with her in mid-June, due to a cancellation. When we arrived for the appointment, we discovered that there had been a mistake in the scheduling; her staff had given our slot to another patient. Her staff then rescheduled us for July 17, the next available time. During the July appointment, we discussed Elizabeth's medical history, test results, and treatment. We will be seeing Dr. K on an annual basis for follow-up to Elizabeth's condition. We discussed the pending court case as well. Dr. K felt that our case had merit, and as a result we worked with her office over the following days to complete the paperwork and payments necessary for initiating her review and developing an expert opinion. Dr. K was out of the office during much of late summer and early fall but managed to get to the case and review all the exhibits submitted. In October, she contacted me by email and informed me, based on her experience, that she did not think there was enough documentation in the medical records to meet the burden of proof that the court requires. She reiterated that another medical professional might have a different opinion.

After performing some short searches, we have not managed to locate any additional experts. This is a highly specialized field, and the few experts who exist have little time to accept new requests. Locating and securing such an expert could take many months. In addition, based on our experience with Dr. K, we have been somewhat shocked at the fees that such experts require. It would be difficult for us to come up with the necessary funds to pay a new expert if we found one.

Because of these issues, we have decided to dismiss

our case now and discuss options for doing so. This is a decision we very much regret. Over the past two and a half years, we have spent considerable time and resources in pursuing this effort. However, we want to be realistic about our prospects and refrain from using the courts time unnecessarily and consuming resources of our own which may be better spent on our daughter's care and treatment.

Thank you,

Again, note the level of detail I go into here. I wanted to make sure the court understood that we worked hard to get the information requested and that we were not making a frivolous case. It's important to make sure the court knows that your case is being filed in good faith and that you are doing everything possible to pursue it to the end.

Once I realized that our chances of obtaining a settlement were over, I was saddled with a lot of expenses. The filing costs and, particularly, all the medical costs due to the muscle biopsy amounted to several thousand dollars. The opposing attorney initially denied paying these costs, and in response, I had to file a pleading explaining our case. Below is an example of such a pleading.

Example of a Pleading

US Court of Federal Claims
Washington, DC 20005
RE: Anon v. HHS, No. 00000
Pleading

Dear Special Master and Opposing Attorney:

Per the order received on February 28, I am providing the following pleading explaining and supporting our position that the muscle biopsy was performed for litigation purposes.

In the summer of 2011 we decided to pursue a

vaccination case for our daughter and began researching the topic. One of the attorneys we spoke with performed some research on our behalf. Attached is the email chain with the result of his research. He contacted another firm with experience in the field, and they came back and said that they were not taking any new cases unless the child had seizures within the proper period resulting in brain damage or the child had a mitochondrial disorder, as proven by muscle biopsy. Since our daughter had not presented with any documented seizures, the only other option per the email was to prove mitochondrial disorder via muscle biopsy. We had good reason to believe that our daughter had mitochondrial disease because some blood tests performed by Dr. L noted a possible mitochondrial problem (see exhibit 5 previously provided to the court). Since he was only a pediatrician skilled in autism disorders, we were referred to a neurologist, Dr. N. Dr. N performed some additional blood tests, but these were inconclusive. I believe the court also has these records. Dr. N referred us to Dr. M, a known expert in mitochondrial disease. He recommended a muscle biopsy and lumbar puncture because these were the only known reliable methods to prove mitochondrial disease. It took us several months of referrals and paperwork to get in to see Dr. M and schedule the surgery. The biopsy was performed in May 2012, the results were available in July 2012 confirming the disease, and we immediately followed with our filing in August.

We ended up filing our case an entire year later than we could have because of the time it took to arrange the testing. As you know, time is precious with these cases, and we were aware of the time lost but were convinced, based on the email, that we had no case without a muscle biopsy.

I hope this information satisfies the court. We plead

that our costs of obtaining the muscle biopsy were incurred for litigation purposes.

Thank you,

This pleading was quickly and handily denied, but I followed with the below reply, which received the response I was looking for.

US Court of Federal Claims
Washington, DC 20005
RE: Anon v. HHS, No. 00000
Reply Pleading

Dear Special Master:

Per the order received on May 16, I am providing the following reply pleading to the Respondent's response to our request for reimbursement of mitochondrial testing.

We (Petitioners) understand that we are not entitled to compensation under U.S.C. 300aa-15(a). We also understand that our request for reimbursement should be covered under section 15(e) of the Vaccine Act. The Respondent states that diagnostic testing is not covered under section 15(e) because "diagnosis" is mentioned in 15(a). However, there is nothing in the statute clearly indicating that compensation under these two sections must always be mutually exclusive based on the *type or nature* of the cost alone. The primary difference between the two is whether they were incurred in any proceeding for the petition. Costs under section 15(a) are deemed "past un-reimbursable expenses" because they were not incurred in pursuit of the claim, as section 15(e) requires, not because they were diagnostic in nature. Further, there is nothing under section 15(e) that precludes specific cost types, such as diagnostic testing, if they can be shown to have been "incurred in any proceeding on such a petition." Reimbursement for attorney's fees and "other costs" can be provided under section 15(e), whether the Petitioners have won their case or not. Indeed, the nature of "*other costs*" under section 15(e) is rather open-ended and is not limited to specific expense types if they were incurred in pursuit of the claim and if such claim was found to be filed in good faith and with reasonable basis.

The Respondent further contends that our "subjective belief" that mitochondrial testing was needed was "erroneous" but provides no documentation or case law proving this to be so. If such a case like ours has been successful without such testing, we would like to see the case reference.

We therefore plead that our request for coverage of the mitochondrial testing under section 15(e) is valid because:

1. "Other costs" under section 15(e) is silent with respect to the nature of the cost and does not explicitly preclude diagnostic testing.
2. As shown in our previous pleading, the testing in question was required by our legal counsel at the time in pursuit of the claim and therefore meets the criteria set forth in section 15(e) as "costs incurred in *any proceeding* on such a petition."
3. The Respondent agrees that the petition was filed in good faith and with reasonable basis. This fact is not under contention and meets the criteria under section 15(e). Indeed, one could argue that performing this testing may have been necessary in establishing such reasonable basis.

In addition, it is important to note that the amount requested of $----- is only the remaining balance owed and does not consider previous payments made by our insurance or by us (Petitioners). These payments can be observed on the bill that the Respondent provided. The original cost of the muscle biopsy surgery and testing was well over $--------.

This briefing is particularly important because you may be in the same position and find yourself trying to get compensation for similar costs. The opposing side tried vigorously to avoid paying this, and my briefing is probably the best argument available. Even the special master complemented me on it, and she was pretty much convinced that I must have had a lawyer help me through this whole process! It's amazing what we can accomplish with the Lord's help. As the Bible says in Proverbs 3:5–6, "Trust in the Lord with all your heart, and do not lean on your own understanding. In all your ways acknowledge him, and he will make straight your paths."

There are a couple of different ways to close your case once you've given it up. These can allow you to pursue the case later if you want and also can protect your privacy.

Lessons Learned

1. I can't emphasize this enough: Closely monitor your medical records regularly. Ask your doctor questions, and document the answers.
2. Work hard to find a sympathetic medical specialist. You won't get far without one.
3. Even though we didn't win our case, we gained knowledge about our daughter's condition that has helped us improve her treatment, and the Lord provided a way to subsidize the cost.
4. Remember the three-year filing limitation! The clock does not begin on the date of diagnosis; it starts upon the presentation of the first symptoms, even if you had no idea the implications of those symptoms at the time.
5. Unless your child has a distinct and acute encephalopathic reaction (severe seizure or similar neurological event) following a vaccination that puts him or her in the hospital, these cases are very hard to

fight. Lawyers and even some doctors only look for the obvious, but I believe that many of these situations present much more subtle symptoms over time. Be observant, and make sure you or your doctor documents everything, no matter how benign it may seem.

12

Mitochondrial Disease

The comment from the DAN! doctor about mitochondria continued to gnaw at me. I had a hunch, or instinct, that a mitochondrial issue was at the root of Elizabeth's autism. I was hopeful that if we could determine this root cause, some sort of treatment could be determined that would help her.

If you have picked up this book, you probably know autism is a neurobiological disorder that affects a person's ability to communicate and relate. Autism is part of a wide spectrum that can be mild, as in Asperger's, or severe, resulting in near mental retardation. The condition is reaching epidemic proportions, affecting children across all racial and ethnic backgrounds. Although it affects boys more often than girls, girls tend to be affected more severely. An underlying diagnosis is obtained in less than a third of autistic cases. Although mitochondrial disease is a rare cause of autism, it is one of the most commonly definable ones.

For autistic concerns, you should start with a neurologist. Your neurologist will conduct a series of tests to try to determine if there are any commonly known genetic abnormalities or insults to the brain. I say "commonly known" because typically your neurologist won't be testing for everything, only a subset of abnormalities. In our case, no problems were found. However, there was a small anomaly with respect to the mitochondria, and even though the doctor did not think it was significant and was doubtful that Elizabeth had any kind of mitochondrial disease, I pushed for answers.

He eventually referred us to two mitochondrial specialists, as I have discussed previously. There are very few of these specialists worldwide, so we were lucky that we had two of them locally. I was unable to get a response from one of the doctors but managed to obtain contact with the other. We then arranged a meeting.

What is mitochondrial disease? Well, to summarize, mitochondria are the power plants of your cells. These mitochondria are comprised of five groups of chemicals that are referred to as "complexes." A problem with any one of these complexes can result in the mitochondria being unable to produce the necessary energy, resulting in disease. These problems are thought to be caused by either a mutation in the genetic blueprint or an external "trigger," such as a medication. Although occurrence of the disease itself is rare, many people are carriers and don't know it. Mitochondria is passed from mother to daughter virtually unchanged, just as the Y chromosome in men is passed from father to son unchanged.

Mitochondrial disease can manifest with a variety of symptoms across many organ systems. These include developmental delays, seizures, autism, and neuro-psychiatric problems. Muscle weakness, hypotonia, and gastrointestinal problems are also common symptoms. Finally, the disease can affect the kidneys, liver, eyes, ears, and heart.

Common clues that young children have this condition are muscle weakness, strabismus, and gastrointestinal issues. If your child seems to be a "floppy baby," with issues sitting up, rolling over, or walking, you should have your child checked. Problems feeding and keeping food down should be investigated. Regular eye and ear checkups should be conducted as well.

There are various types of mitochondrial disease, such as Leigh's disease, complex I, complex IV, etc. I won't get into the various types, as they vary widely, and knowledge regarding them is constantly changing. I will say that autistic children with mitochondrial disease tend to be a bit more resilient than typical children who have the condition. Prognosis for children affected with mito, as it is commonly called, is widely varied but typically progresses over time. The truth is that your child can die young due to this condition, which is a specter we live with on a daily basis. Losing your child to autism is bad enough, but losing him or her altogether is something else.

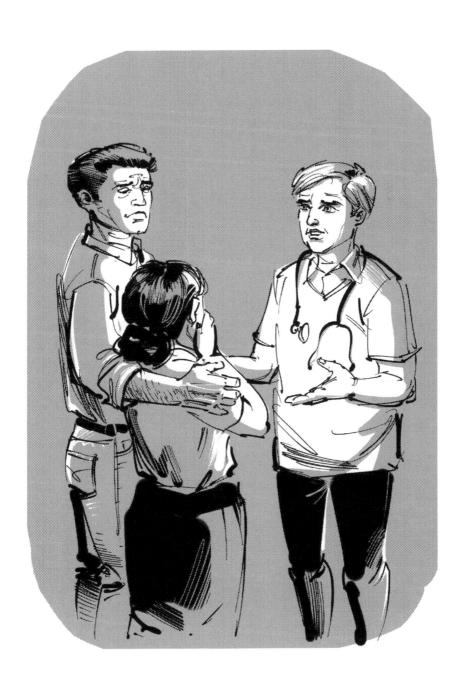

As the Bible says in Romans 5:1–21, "Therefore, since we have been justified by faith, we have peace with God through our Lord Jesus Christ. Through him we have also obtained access by faith into this grace in which we stand, and we rejoice in hope of the glory of God. More than that, we rejoice in our sufferings, knowing that suffering produces endurance, and endurance produces character, and character produces hope, and hope does not put us to shame, because God's love has been poured into our hearts through the Holy Spirit who has been given to us."

The condition can worsen if the child is under stress, such as sickness or surgery, so it's important to keep these to a minimum as much as possible. Regression after some of these episodes is common. Be on the lookout for fevers, diarrhea, or vomiting.

Treatment involves taking care of the symptoms as much as possible. Early detection is critical, because the sooner you institute proper care, the better. That's why if you believe your child may have mitochondrial disease or another underlying condition causing your child's autism, you need to pursue it. Go with your gut. It could save or at least prolong the quality of your child's life. Therapeutics are very limited. There isn't really any medication that helps the underlying condition itself, so as I mentioned before, the emphasis is on treating the symptoms. Some supplements have been proven to help the condition somewhat, including CoQ10. However, supplements like these are often very expensive (for good quality and highly absorbable products) and are not typically covered under most insurance plans. In our case, we could not determine if the CoQ10 was doing any good or not, so we stopped it.

The doctor we were put in touch with initially emphasized that the condition could only be definitively diagnosed via a muscle biopsy and lumbar puncture. Since we were told that this was also required to support our daughter's legal case, we agreed to proceed. Getting insurance coverage required a lot of paperwork, but the doctor's office assured us they were taking care of it. Approval seemed to take forever, but once we achieved it, we agonized over going through with it. We hated the idea of Elizabeth going through surgery, but we wanted desperately to help her, and my gut was telling me that the procedure would provide some answers. She went through the surgery like a champ, with no problems at all. The results gave us mixed emotions. On the one hand, my gut instincts were proven correct. She had the condition, and at last we knew what the underlying cause of her autism was. The bad news was that she had mitochondrial disease, a much more serious diagnosis than autism itself. I was hopeful that this new diagnosis would help us in some way and result in better treatment options. This is all true, of course, but treatment and management of the condition is severely limited.

Below is a list of questions that we asked our doctor upon diagnosis. I do not include the answers here, because every child is different, and there are various types of mitochondrial disease. If you find yourself in a similar position, this list could serve as a guide for what to ask when discussing the condition with your doctor. I am often frustrated with how short doctors' visits are, and it's sometimes difficult to get all my questions answered unless I am prepared. I try to make the most of these visits, and you should too.

Questions to Ask Your Doctor

1. Does this report indicate that my child has mitochondrial disease?
   a. We're aware that there are many variations of mitochondrial disease. Does my child have a specific kind (Leigh's disease, etc.)?
2. How serious is this?
   a. Is it life threatening? Will my child die?
   b. What is his or her life expectancy?
3. The report indicates that the disease is isolated to the central nervous system.
   a. Can it spread?
   b. If so, how fast?
4. Will my child's condition become progressively worse?
   a. If so, how fast?
   b. What are the symptoms or indicators of this progression?
5. What is my child's prognosis?
6. What kind of impact can we expect from the supplements being recommended?
   a. Will they slow or stop the progression?
   b. Can you advise on the best pharmacy to obtain them?

    c. Is Medicaid accepted?

7.   There is still further testing to be done.

    a. Can you tell us the nature of this additional testing?

    b. Has it been approved by our insurance yet? If not, how much longer will that take?

    c. Does this additional "gene sequencing" require more surgery?

    d. What new information will this testing provide?

8.   My child is a picky eater. Lately my child has become a little more picky and will eat only a select number of foods. We are worried that he or she may have trouble swallowing or have acid reflux. Can you advise?

    a. Should we see a specialist?

    b. Is this a cause for concern?

    c. Is this a key disease symptom or perhaps just a phase?

9.   We've read that this disease often affects the eyes. My child has been seeing an ophthalmologist annually and has a good report.

    a. Should we change anything we're doing?

    b. Should we add supplements?

    c. Should we have more frequent checkups?

10. Do you treat mitochondrial disease or just diagnose it?

    a. Can you refer us to a mitochondrial specialist for treatment?

11. We are concerned about our child's nutrition. Can you advise?

12. Our child currently takes a variety of supplements prescribed by a DAN! (or functional medicine) doctor. We would like you to review these for interactions with anything you need him or her to take.

13. Could this impact future children if we have any?

    a. If so, what are the chances of having another child with this condition?

14. Was this caused by vaccinations?

15. What kind of clinical trials are available or in the works?

    a. What is the success rate so far?

16. Are there any experimental treatments?

17. What is the current state of research in this area?

18. Who are the most progressive/aggressive researchers and/or experts?

19. What else can we do as parents?

20. Will ABA therapy still help our child?

21. Will OT/PT/speech therapy still help our child?
22. Should therapy be increased?
23. Is there an additional type of therapy or technique that is better for our child's condition?

Our doctor proposed an array of supplements and additional testing to gauge the progress of the disease, including, most importantly, the highly concentrated versions of CoQ10. Therapies, including ABA, occupational, and speech, were and often are recommended. Follow-ups are typically handled on an annual basis.

We had full confidence in this doctor and were initially happy with the care, even though scheduling appointments could sometimes be difficult. The only negative aspect of this doctor was the doctor's staff, who were often rude, rotated frequently, and were disorganized. Good doctors don't always make the best business managers. As it turned out, the staff had missed a filing deadline with the insurance company, and as a result, the costs came out of our pockets. Fortunately, we were able to recoup our costs through the court at a much later date. Although this doctor had a full-service practice for mitochondrial disease, he was focused mostly on the laboratory and research facility that he controlled, and eventually he closed his practice to managing patients.

The good news is that we were lucky enough to find another local doctor who specialized in mito and focused on patient care. Our new doctor didn't believe a muscle biopsy was necessary to diagnose the disease and that diagnosis could be performed with less invasive means. It was too late for us, but this is something for you to keep in mind when making your decisions regarding which avenue to pursue. Annual visits consisted of more thorough physical examinations and detailed recommendations, as opposed to just laboratory results and analysis. We were given an entire protocol to share with the school and therapists so that they could all be on the same page. We also went through some additional genetic testing on my wife and me to help determine if there were any links or if more details around the diagnosis could be determined. We were hopeful that this could shed more light on the condition and perhaps link us to some upcoming clinical trials. Nothing was found, but our information is included in a database that will be used to find links as further discoveries develop. New findings regarding mitochondrial disease and related conditions are being found all the time. It is possible that such findings could link us to clinical trials for new treatments as they become available.

One new development is medical cannabis. This is a bit controversial, but it has proven to provide results, especially in children with seizures or behavioral issues. We have not tried this yet, because we are waiting for state laws to catch up with the medical research. However, once it does, it is something we may consider. We turn to Revelation 22:2 for comfort: "Through the middle of the street of the city; also, on either side of the river, the tree of life with its twelve kinds of fruit, yielding its fruit each month. The leaves of the tree were for the healing of the nations."

Lessons Learned

1. Don't ignore your instincts. Listen to your gut. All our doctors dismissed the mitochondrial angle until we pursued it.
2. Look for doctors who are patient-focused. Remember those professors in college who were so consumed with research that they ignored their students? If your doctor is distracted with laboratories or other sidelines, this could affect your care. Keep looking if you can, although in some specializations options are limited.
3. Find the underlying cause of your child's autism if you can. I spoke with one parent who "didn't want to know" and said "it didn't matter." That's crazy. Finding out the cause could improve the quality of your life as well as your child's.
4. Fight hard. This relates to number 3 above. Don't give up. We fought hard for our child in the courts, in the schools, with insurance companies, and in doctors' offices. You should too. By the way, we are still fighting.

13

Feeding Problems, Bad Behaviors, and Worries

Parents always worry about their children. However, special-needs children cause worries beyond compare. First, there are the long-term concerns. Who will take care of your child after you are gone? How will your child live? What will your child do? What will your child's life be like? Who will love your child? Thinking about these subjects can cause you to lose a lot of sleep at night. I've mentioned some of this before including the following scriptures, but it bears repeating here because worry can be so overwhelming with regards to our little ones. Many of these problems are out of your control and should be left in God's hands. There are many scriptures on this topic:

> Do not be anxious about anything, but in everything by prayer and supplication with thanksgiving let your requests be made known to God. And the peace of God, which surpasses all understanding, will guard your hearts and your minds in Christ Jesus. (Philippians 4:6–7)

> Therefore I tell you, do not be anxious about your life, what you will eat or what you will drink, nor about your body, what you will put on. Is not life more than food, and the body more than clothing? Look at the birds of the air: they neither sow nor reap nor gather into barns,

and yet your heavenly Father feeds them. Are you not of more value than they? And which of you by being anxious can add a single hour to his span of life? And why are you anxious about clothing? Consider the lilies of the field, how they grow: they neither toil nor spin, yet I tell you, even Solomon in all his glory was not arrayed like one of these. (Matthew 6:25–34)

Casting all your anxieties on him, because he cares for you. (1 Peter 5:7)

But seek first the kingdom of God and his righteousness, and all these things will be added to you. "Therefore do not be anxious about tomorrow, for tomorrow will be anxious for itself. Sufficient for the day is its own trouble. (Matthew 6:33–34)

Despite the long-term ramifications of a special-needs child, most of us are embroiled with more immediate concerns. Mitochondrial disease is a degenerative one, and so in Elizabeth's case, we were worried as to how this would manifest. Our mitochondrial specialist was mostly silent on the topic. Some children start to have problems early, while others do not have problems until later. Some children die young, while others live to adulthood. There was just no way to know. If there was, our doctor did not say anything. We have often observed that specialists make value judgments about what to tell you and what not to tell. These doctors see a lot of these children and have a pretty good idea of how the condition progresses. However, it is also true that all children are different. If you sense that you are being goldbricked, you can press your doctor for more information. However, the truth is they simply don't know, and anything they tell you is just an educated guess. We all know that God is the only true physician in these situations, so we recommend prayer: "Bless the Lord, O my soul, and forget not all his benefits, who forgives all your iniquity, who heals all your diseases" (Psalm 103:2–3).

We came to the realization that our child does not have an expiration date on her, so we work every day to lean on our faith, especially when it comes to longer term worries. Despite this, we are always on the lookout for any possible problems or signs. Lack of energy, frequent illness, and lack of growth or appetite are the main things we watch for.

Most autistic children are picky eaters, and Elizabeth was one of them. However, she managed to get enough and maintain herself. Her growth was good. Her pediatrician said that although many children are picky eaters, they seem to get enough to eat somehow through their own little ways. This continued for a few years, until she reached second grade. This is when she began turning away food items that she typically ate and started to look skinny. Her doctors noted that although she was still on track based on the height/weight growth scale, she was moving toward the bottom in terms of her weight. Her pediatrician was not that worried, but our psychologist and mito specialist were. Our biggest worry was that this represented some kind of gastrointestinal issue. We thought that maybe the mitochondrial disease was interfering with her digestion. She seemed to have a lot of gas and would sometimes appear to choke on her food. We visited a pediatric gastrointestinal doctor briefly who was no help at all. We then visited a food therapist at the local autism center who thought that Elizabeth's problem was based in an oral sensitivity rather than a gastrointestinal problem. Her mito specialist told us that if Elizabeth did not start eating better, she might have to be put on a feeding tube. We worried and fretted over this for quite some time, trying to figure out whether Elizabeth had a serious gastrointestinal issue that was indicating the beginning of the end or if it was something not nearly as serious. Her psychologist prescribed a medication that would stimulate her appetite, but the school complained that it caused behavioral problems. We spent each day monitoring Elizabeth's eating closely. Each meal was a task. What will she eat? How much? What else can we try? She would often reject her solid meals and gravitate toward junk foods. We didn't like to see her eat potato chips and crackers, but to an extent, we were glad just to see her eat something.

During the winter, Elizabeth came down with a stomach bug and had some diarrhea. She again wouldn't eat. Her doctor sent her to the hospital for fluids and to get something in her. This was our first hospital visit with Elizabeth since her birth, and it deeply upset us. I was also ill with ulcerative colitis at the time, so it did not do me any good either. The doctors tried several times to contact our mito specialist for direction, but to my knowledge they never got a response. Elizabeth was kept overnight; they got some intravenous fluids in her, and we got her to eat. We were scared to death that they would recommend putting a stomach plug in her, something that we felt would be the beginning of the end for our little girl. Fortunately, they were encouraged enough by what little she ate to send her home. She did look much better after being brought back from such dehydration. At home, we immediately started giving her the appetite medication. Her eating improved, and she started gaining weight. We got Elizabeth set up with a feeding therapist a few times a week. This therapist gave us some valuable information about something I mentioned earlier, "food jagging," which is when autistic kids get used to eating the same thing for a long time and then suddenly quit eating it because they can't stand it anymore. Often such children will stop eating what used to be their favorite foods for as long as a year. We noticed that Elizabeth's choking was not choking at all; it was gagging. She had some oral issue that caused her to want to break her food up into small pieces.

As it turns out, Elizabeth's feeding problems are the result of food jagging and oral sensitivity and have nothing to do with any serious gastrointestinal or degenerative mitochondrial issue. Her feeding continues to improve, and she is growing and gaining weight. I praise God for this victory.

Be sure to praise God for each little victory you have with your child! With special-needs children, it is often the little victories that count. Be diligent about following up and getting to the root of your child's issues. Often you must be your own doctor. Most of all, have faith that it will all work out. As it says in the scriptures, "Heal me, O Lord, and I shall be healed; save me, and I shall be saved, for you are my praise" (Jeremiah 12:14).

Another challenging issue with autistic children is bad behavior. Bad behaviors can range from mild tantrums to severe meltdowns in which the child physically injures himself or herself and takes a long time to calm down. These can be rare or frequent and can translate into other problems, such as sleeping issues, lack of focus at school, and the parents' inability to take the child anywhere.

Elizabeth had always slept pretty well, and her tantrums varied. She had a pacifier addiction, which we had tried to break a few times. We tried giving her a "bunny," which was a small rubber figure, and then a "chew stick" for her to transition to. Unfortunately, instead of letting alone the pacifier and moving to the other objects, she started carrying all three around at the same time. We did manage to keep her from needing them at school, but once she got home she just had to have them. Most professionals, and indeed pretty much everyone, will tell you to simply take these items away cold turkey; the child will fuss a while but eventually adapt. We tried this approach beginning with bunny, because he was the easiest. Bunny tended to wear out, losing bits and pieces of himself. Each time he was misplaced, he became more difficult to find. Bunny lost his arms, legs, ears, and eventually disappeared. One down, two to go!

We finally decided to take the pacifier away entirely. "Da Pwug," as she often referred to it, was gone. Her grandfather would often pick at her and grab the pacifier away saying, "Take that plug outta your mouth!" That's where the name originated. The first few days without the "pwug" were great; there was a little fussing but not much resistance. This began to change when she had school break and spent more time at home with a different routine. Autistic children are often quite attached to their routines, and when these change for some reason, it can cause havoc. We noticed that Elizabeth started having trouble sleeping, a problem she never had before. She started getting up at all hours of the night, asking for snacks or wanting to play. One time she ran into our room in the middle of the night and pounced on me like a wildcat. She grabbed my mouth to get my attention and asked for "pwug." Her getting up at night transitioned into having tantrums at all hours, and so the condition got even worse.

Sleep may have been the worst part, but it didn't end there. Elizabeth started developing issues riding in the car. Every time we came to a stoplight she would have a tantrum and even pull her hair to the point of yanking it out. Not only were we not getting any sleep, but we were also virtually unable to transport her anywhere. At this point, we gave her the "pwug" and "chew" back, thinking that we needed to try a different therapeutic approach to break her from these addictions. She started sleeping soundly almost immediately, but the problems in the car did not change. We hired therapists to go on "rides" with us to help observe and advise on how to deal with her issues, and we also worked with our doctors. I noticed that Elizabeth never had a tantrum when I had to stop to make left turns. I wondered why. She got upset in traffic and virtually every time we had to stop. The only difference was that when I stopped for a left turn, I used my signal, which made a "tick tock" sound. I figured that this sound had some kind of calming effect on her. Whenever we got stuck in severe traffic, I would turn on my hazards, and suddenly Elizabeth would get quiet again. This helped for a while and, combined with the advice from our therapists and doctors, eventually eliminated the behavior. It took time and patience, however, and there were times when we thought it would never get better, but it did. The bad news is that we lost this battle. In the end, Elizabeth still had her "pwug." Mom and Dad were forced to respect the pacifier, at least for the time being.

We still struggle with breaking Elizabeth from bad behaviors. New behaviors come and go, and old behaviors we thought eliminated pop up again. The best we can do is work with our doctors and therapists to manage these issues and hopefully eliminate them as she gets older.

Lessons Learned

1. Consult with your doctors, but do your due diligence and make your own decisions. You know your child best. In our case, our psychiatrist, pediatrician, gastroenterologist, and mito specialist all told us something different. We had to take the information given to us and make the best decision.

2. A conservative approach generally works best. You need to go with your gut on this one, but most of the time I've found that the most conservative approach to treatment is the best route to take. Avoid unnecessary surgeries, procedures, and drugs at all cost.

3. Don't worry about the worst-case scenario until it happens. It's been said that most of what we worry about never happens. This may be

an old, tired cliché, but it's true. Don't be ignorant about the worst-case scenario, but it should not be your primary or even tertiary concern.

4. Be positive when bad behaviors arise. It *will* get better, no matter how bad it seems at the time.

5. The future is in God's hands. Plan for your child as best as you can. Apply for all available government assistance. Create a trust fund. Consult with friends and family to design a care plan. Do what you can on this earth to help your child, but remember that in the end, it's all in God's hands.

14

Family

When you have a disabled child, you will find that your need for family assistance is greater than ever. The day-to-day workload can be daunting and exhausting. You also need to make time for yourself and your spouse, and having some family assistance will be critical to making that happen. If you come from a large yet close-knit family, consider yourself lucky. Many parents may not have much family to turn to, at least not anyone available and healthy enough to contribute. The problem, though, is that family members often have a hard time understanding autism and its day-to-day impacts. Relatives may give advice instead of lending a helping hand.

In addition to our daily experiences, my wife and I attended numerous training courses and support sessions with various therapists and experts. After years of training, we have become very knowledgeable in dealing with our daughter's issues. However, there are problems, and not every technique works all the time. We are always learning, and our child's conditions and issues are always changing.

Autism is easy for relatives to dismiss. Since they only come for short visits, what they see is a perfectly fine-looking child who has behavior problems. It's tempting for such relatives to classify such a child as unruly, spoiled, or uncontrolled. Often, they are convinced that *they* can fix the child, which results in disaster. More than once we've had relatives offer to babysit Elizabeth for several days while we went on a trip, only to have them completely fall apart into a sobbing mess by the time we returned. But even after these experiences, the same relatives often didn't completely learn their lesson.

A second problem with relatives, as mentioned above, is that they tend to provide advice instead of a helping hand. It was so frustrating to us when people would shoot things out of their mouths with no training, knowledge, or experience with the condition whatsoever, and then they'd just sit there and do nothing while we suffered. My advice to relatives of a disabled child, especially autistic ones, is *shut up and lend a hand*. If you cannot help with the child, help with other things around the house. There is so much that people can do if they truly want to help someone who is suffering. The last thing you need to do is try to provide answers to questions that even the experts cannot tackle.

The third problem is a lack of empathy. Most relatives just have no idea how bad it really is on a day-to-day basis. Many people must experience something themselves before they understand it. They aren't capable of empathic cognition or reasoning. As a result, when you call relatives for moral support, all you get is lectures or advice or people minimizing your pain: "Aw, that's nothing. That's not so bad. Get over it." This can make you feel belittled and angry. My advice to relatives in this situation is that when a suffering parent calls you, he or she is looking for a shoulder to cry on. The parent needs encouragement, sympathy, and love. What he or she doesn't need are lectures or belittlement of their concerns or their child's condition. Trying to make a parent's concerns seem like nothing insults their intelligence.

Here are my rules for extended family of autistic children:

1. Empathize. It's hard to put yourself in someone else's shoes, but try to imagine what the parents of these children are going through. They are set up for a lifetime of uncertainty, not knowing what will become of their child, whether the disease will get worse and when, and how they will manage the constant day-to-day struggles.

2. Know your limitations. Unless you are a professional or have gone through what the parents have gone through, your advice should be kept to yourself.

3. Lend a hand. You're not going to solve this problem, so chip in and help any way possible. Talk is cheap. Help and love are worth their weight in gold to a parent struggling to care for a child and keep up with daily affairs or a job.

4. Listen, love, and nurture. Parents of these children need love and understanding. They have their weak times and will need a shoulder to cry on. Just listen, empathize, and love them. Strengthen them. Don't tear them down with criticism. Love and nurture. Build them up rather than break them down. It may make you feel good to blame someone, such as the parents, but it does not help.

For parents in this situation, try to understand that relatives, especially your own parents, only want the best for you and are trying to help, even if their efforts are having the opposite effect. Try to be patient and understanding, and educate them. Recognize that relatives, especially grandparents, can be your biggest advocate and resource if groomed properly. These are very complex conditions that are difficult for even professionals to fully understand, so don't expect grandparents to become experts overnight. Don't cut the cord, don't sever the relationship, but do work at it. As Exodus 12:12 says, "Honor your father and your mother, that your days may be prolonged in the land which the Lord your God gives you."

15

Special Schools

Once Elizabeth was diagnosed, we were eager to get her into a regular program. We had always been told that early intervention is critical for long-term success. I still believe that. The earlier you can get your child the help he or she needs, or at least some help, the better off your child will be. For a while, we had in-home ABA therapy for about nine hours per week. We knew it wasn't enough, and it certainly wasn't cost effective. The results were somewhat dubious as well. We researched several programs and came across one at a local university that seemed to be the best fit. Getting accepted into some of these programs isn't easy. There are lengthy evaluation processes and limitations on the numbers and types of children that can be accepted, and of course, they are all very expensive.

Ultimately, Elizabeth was accepted into the university program. The biggest downside was the location, which was a very long commute from our home. My wife would have to make drives early in the mornings and then back again in the afternoons, all during rush hour traffic. Not to mention that the school had strict rules about arrival and departure times. They don't like to start late and certainly don't like to have to babysit your child while you fight traffic in the afternoon. We had to make some changes, one of which was to get a smaller and more efficient car that could handle the commutes.

Despite the logistical challenges, we heard nothing but good things about the program and figured it was worth it. We liked the staff and their approach. They mixed "typical" children in with autistic children, which helped integrate them into regular classrooms. They also gathered statistics on each child's progress and integrated this into their research. We hoped that this would bring about greater insights into Elizabeth's condition, abilities, and how we could better deal with her issues.

Elizabeth's first teacher was a determined young man. The first thing he wanted to work on was potty training. We were worried about that. We had heard and seen horror stories about children getting up in years, never being potty trained, and still wearing diapers well into grade school. We had no idea how to go about such training with a special-needs child. However, this guy was determined, and he told us that Elizabeth *would* be potty trained. We loved his confidence and determination. We did have to do some homework to make it happen. We had to make Elizabeth sit on the potty at certain times and use a timer to make sure she stayed there. The intervals of introducing her to the potty and the timings for her to stay on it were gradually reduced. As was typical for most children her age, we started with a small plastic potty before moving her to the toilet. I still remember her first successful potty and how excited we all were. Sure enough, it did not take long for Elizabeth to become potty trained. She initiated and went all by herself. She still needed help cleaning herself and pulling up her pants, but the fact that she could go on her own and did not need diapers was a monumental achievement for her. We were so happy and proud!

The next goal was to work on speaking. This started with communicating wants and needs. Our hope was that this would eliminate a lot of the frustration that Elizabeth had. Communication usually starts with hand signals; one of the more popular ones was "more." Elizabeth could use her hands to tell us she wanted more juice or more food. She could also indicate to us exactly what she wanted, using gestures. But it wasn't long before she started using her voice. I still remember the first time that Elizabeth asked for a cookie, plain as day. It was remarkable! "I want a cookie, please!" By the end of the year, Elizabeth could communicate basic wants verbally and go to the potty. In addition to this, she started singing! "Wheels on the Bus" was her favorite song (and she loves singing it still today). We were so excited! In just one year she had made remarkable progress.

The following year, we brought Elizabeth back to the same university program. This year she got a different teacher, a young lady with a large mop of curly hair. This person seemed always downtrodden and had a bad attitude. She never smiled and seemed negative and sad all the time. We watched her in the classroom through the one-way observation window a few times and noted the frown on her face. We also noticed that Elizabeth was becoming increasingly agitated and was missing hair. She never pulled her hair at home, so we weren't sure what was happening. After attending another observation, we saw Elizabeth being held down in one of the instructors' laps as she had a tantrum and pulled her hair. Elizabeth did not make as much progress the second year, which is when her long saga of self-injury and hair pulling started.

I can't emphasize enough how much of a difference the teacher makes. No matter how good the school may be, or its methodology, or its leadership, it comes down to who is sitting with your child in the classroom. That is what makes all the difference in the world. These children are also very sensitive; they can tell when someone isn't sincere about helping them. If the instructor shows sincerity and love, the child picks up on it, and it makes a huge difference. The right teacher can help your child grow in leaps and bounds, whereas the wrong teacher can result in long-term stagnation and neglect.

School leadership is often clueless about instructors' performance. It is all too easy to dismiss low performance as being the child's fault. School administrators often think that parents are looking for a silver bullet or are setting their expectations too high. "Parents expect us to *fix* their child" is a mantra we have heard over and over again for years from teachers. We know our child is disabled, but we're paying a lot of money, and we know our child. We can tell if her problems are organic or are being exacerbated by outside influences. It also doesn't take an expert to figure out that if the child progresses dramatically one year and falters the next, there's got to be some environmental factors involved. But again, school administrators often dismiss such things, because these children change and sometimes do acquire new problems and challenges as they get older.

We enjoyed our time at the university program and believed it was an excellent place to bring Elizabeth. But given the last year's results, we decided that we couldn't afford to bring her back the following year. It was time for public school.

16

Public School

After spending so long in private instruction we were apprehensive about public school. We heard all the horror stories: autistic children not being cared for, are being neglected, and are even being abused. Even in our own county, there had been news reports of teachers duct-taping an autistic child to a chair to control him. We were so fearful, but we just couldn't afford private instruction any longer. We were tax-paying citizens, and it was time that our daughter got the benefits.

The good news is that most of our fears were unfounded. During the evaluation process, the school had several therapists, including physical, occupational, speech, and other professionals, evaluate Elizabeth. We could tell that they had a passion for disabled children, and a couple of them seemed to fall in love with Elizabeth right away. One therapist even wept as Elizabeth tried to sing "Wheels on the Bus." When she was asked her name, she would say "Wizabit" in a very quiet voice. At this point, "Wizabit," as we often called her, had her head shaved because of her hair-pulling issues, and she looked both pitiful and extremely cute at the same time. Her little ears seemed to come to a point and stick out at the tips beside her rounded head, which was covered in thin fur. All you wanted to do was kiss her as she looked up at you with those big baby blues.

We reviewed the findings and recommendations for the IEP (individualized educational program) with the evaluators, principal, and teacher at Elizabeth's new school. This school was not her permanent neighborhood school, but it was the closest with an autism class for children Elizabeth's age (pre-k). The following year she would age out and go to a class in her local school. We were very happy with the initial IEP. Fearing the worst, we had hired an "advocate" to attend the session with us. She admitted that she didn't really earn her pay, because it was the easiest IEP meeting she had ever attended. Elizabeth got hours of physical, speech, and occupational therapy. We were so relieved. However, little did we know that this would change once Elizabeth moved to her local school the following year.

Elizabeth had a good start that year and a wonderful teacher. However, we were still leery of public school and had managed to get Elizabeth admitted part-time at a renowned autism center in our city. She attended school part of the week and the autism center for the rest of the week. Our experience at the autism center is another story altogether; I'll return to it in the next chapter.

When it came time for kindergarten, we had to move to the neighborhood school. The new teacher was not as personable as her previous one had been, but she seemed to take a genuine interest in the children's education. We felt confident that she could help Elizabeth learn. Almost from the get-go the new therapy staff began to fail us. The physical therapist demanded that we eliminate physical therapy altogether, as she felt Elizabeth did not need it and that there were "other children who need it more." Other therapists began not showing up at the IEP meetings and asking for "dismissals." Most alarmingly, Elizabeth was sent home with letters on several occasions about being bitten by a classmate, which seemed to be an almost regular occurrence. After a few months, we noticed little fingerprint-sized bruises all over Elizabeth's legs. At one point, one of our doctors pointed it out and voiced concern. We knew Elizabeth was a bit clumsy and would knock her legs around on desks or tables, so we didn't think much of it. We did notice that the bruises looked suspiciously like fingerprints, and I remembered that the teacher had casually mentioned once that they used "pressure points" to control Elizabeth. This is the practice of squeezing or pinching the student with one's fingers to make him or her behave or sit still. When Elizabeth got a new teacher the following year, the bruises disappeared and never recurred.

The kindergarten teacher left because she had a brain issue, and then she moved to work at another school. She eventually had to retire. We were delighted to hear that the new teacher for first grade would be Heather, the same teacher Elizabeth had had in her pre-k class. There was another parent who was glad to hear this news as well. During first grade, this teacher showed much love and care for Elizabeth and the other students. Children in this situation respond very well to positive reinforcement. It's critical that they work in a nurturing environment; it makes all the difference. I can't stress enough how important love is to your child, not just at home but in school as well. If your teaching staff does not have that love and caring spirit for children with special needs, they will not flourish and will become even worse. The Bible warns, "Fathers, do not provoke your children, lest they become discouraged" (Colossians 3:21).

Heather was a great teacher, but she too left after her first year. The next year was the absolute worst. The new teacher was well qualified on paper, and our initial conversation at the beginning of the year went well. However, she turned out to be harsh and impatient. She did not know how to get the best from her students, and she didn't seem to even have the basic skills most special-needs teachers have with regard to reading these children to figure out if they understand things. Elizabeth's progress plummeted, and many of the milestones she'd reached the previous year were deemed unachieved by the new teacher. As egregious as this was, the school blew it off with no explanation other than "different teachers see things differently."

I finally consulted an attorney about the issue. After reviewing the records, they were fully incensed and in complete agreement that there was a problem with the school. They suggested we call an IEP meeting and request a reevaluation of Elizabeth. I got some good information from the attorney, but the cost was astronomical and the rewards too blurry to suit me. We had limited funds and wanted to concentrate our resources to get the most bang for the buck, which meant focusing on Elizabeth's care first and litigation second. However, I followed through on some of the recommendations.

We called an IEP meeting, and again some of the therapists didn't want to stay; I made them stay. I let my displeasure be known. I demanded a reevaluation. However, I didn't follow through with it, because I sensed that they would use it as an opportunity to screw us over and take away the services that Elizabeth had already been awarded, so I never signed the paper approving it. They were all too eager to do the evaluation.

During this school year, we noticed that Elizabeth was losing weight. She was becoming alarmingly skinny. I realized, all too late of course, that the reason was because the new teacher wasn't allowing Elizabeth enough time to eat. We paid for both breakfast and lunch, but Elizabeth wasn't getting any of it. This had not been a problem in previous years because the teachers always worked with her. She got so skinny that her doctors thought they might have to put a feeding tube in her stomach to get nourishment in her. Elizabeth's school was not only neglecting her education, but they were also slowly killing her. Jesus warns, "See that you do not despise one of these little ones, for I say to you that their angels in heaven continually see the face of My Father who is in heaven" (Matthew 18:10).

We found that many other parents in the area had a problem with this particular school and its administration, including another little girl in Elizabeth's class. The writing was on the wall. We had to get our daughter out of there, no matter the cost. So we set about looking for another private school, hoping that somehow the Lord would provide us with the way to pay for it. Ironically, a year later the teacher who had lost two students at the same time was made teacher of the year. Some schools and teachers prefer to eliminate challenging students and focus on the "easy ones" to improve their statistics.

17

Finding Another Special School

During pre-k, Elizabeth had been attending an autism center on a part-time basis. We had worked with this center on a few previous occasions, which included some feeding therapy and parental training. Although this autism center was renowned within the community, our own experiences were problematic and, at best, peculiar. Getting services through the center seemed extremely difficult. There was a gauntlet of paperwork that had to be worked through, for one. We were always told about the high demand and number of students involved, but we later discovered that there were more reasons. Much of the support the autism center offered was in the form of community outreach, which, although nice, was not especially helpful. We were smart enough to read books and train ourselves without a lot of assistance. Most of the time when we called on the center, we were steered away from the school or teaching part of it and redirected to some form of community service. After weeks of wrangling, we got Elizabeth admitted on a part-time basis. It wasn't long before the administrator of the program, Dr. T, said that Elizabeth wasn't the same child she had seen in the evaluations and that she wouldn't make it there. Dr. T went on to tell us essentially that Elizabeth would get worse and worse if we didn't get her behavior under control and that she would end up in some kind of special home when she was an adult. Dr. T warned that she would be unable to ever find employment or enjoy a nice quality of life. We had visions of Elizabeth sitting in a padded room with a straightjacket on, spending her adult life looking out a small slit of a window, with nothing but bread to eat and water to drink. After six short months, Elizabeth was kicked out of the autism center, never to return.

Supposedly the team there had taken a ton of notes, conducted research, and even supplied videos for us to watch. We asked repeatedly for these things. Eventually, one of the therapists did consult with Elizabeth's kindergarten teacher to turn over some information, and she was able to do another ABELLS assessment. We were comfortable with the continuity. We often heard bad things about Dr. T, how she would threaten some parents with dismissing their kids if they didn't behave or do as expected. She made a conscious effort to admit only the "easy students" who were not severely autistic and who were high-functioning on the spectrum. We could only dream of our child being high-functioning. In other words, although this autism center was billed as a school for autistic children, the truth was that most students going there had nothing more than mild learning disabilities, Asperger's, or very mild forms of autism. It was important for them to report "successes" to their donors and investors, and children like our Elizabeth tended to skew their reports. We asked several times for the videos and eventually only got a few short minutes of footage, which was hard to watch. It showed Elizabeth being held down on the "tomato chair," a big red beanbag, by a large and overweight woman, while Elizabeth cried out for her "mama." Elizabeth at this age never said "mama." She must have been under some real stress to do that. To this day, my wife has never watched the video and refuses to do so. Dr. T left the autism center a short time later.

Going back there was not an option. The commute to downtown was horrible anyway. We felt blessed that there seemed to be several options available to us locally. There were quite a few schools for autistic children. However, a couple of them did not take children as severe as Elizabeth. One such school took our one-hundred-dollar application fee and then gave us a quick tour. We were greeted by children brought out of their classrooms to give us a sense of the progress they were making. I noticed that on the walls were paintings and artwork created by the children and being sold for profit and that the school had many corporate sponsors. Money was the game there, which meant only admitting students who wouldn't skew their statistics. Elizabeth was walked out as fast as she walked in, and our application fee was never returned.

We considered a couple of smaller schools, usually those with one or two teachers. These schools also only took children with mild learning disabilities or Asperger's, although they were often billed as autism schools. Autism is a condition with a wide spectrum of severity. It's important that you find out up front what kind of children the school usually takes. It will save you a lot of time and aggravation. Elizabeth was openly stressed about being taken around to different schools. Although her reaction was severe, with a lot of acting out, most children would not be happy about the prospect of moving schools and leaving their comfort zone. Again, calling and talking in depth with someone will save time if the school will let you. Often, the school staff will insist on having you pay an application fee and bringing your child in no matter what. That's a warning sign.

We ended up narrowing our choice down to three schools, all of which would have been pretty good. We cut one school, which we refer to as the "S" center, because they had moved further away from our house, and we had a few bad references on them. For example, we heard one story about a teenage girl like Elizabeth who was punching holes in the walls there. She had attended the place for years, since she was small, and nothing had gotten better for her. That was all we needed to hear. We left and didn't come back.

The two schools left were very good, and one would have been about as good as the other. Both were close to home and had good reputations. One school was newer and cheaper than the other, but to be honest we didn't hear about it in time. We had already paid a lot of money for the initial evaluation at "JL" and didn't want to lose our investment. JL gave parents a wonderful presentation and introduction to the school, preaching love and nurturing. We knew that this was exactly what Elizabeth needed. We believed that she would flourish in this environment. Unfortunately, it was expensive. They all were. We had Elizabeth attend a summer camp at the second school we considered, and she did very well there too. Both were good options. But in the end, we already had an investment in JL, it was practically next door, and it had a good reputation. My own uncle knew the owner and recommended it. We prepared for Elizabeth to attend, and thanks to the Lord, family members were willing to help us with the financing. We were optimistic about Elizabeth making more progress.

18

Finding the Right Church

Before Elizabeth was born, Debbie and I had become members of a large, local church with over twelve thousand members. Although it was difficult to build personal relationships in such a large church, the pastor was a dynamic and charismatic speaker. His sermons and the knowledge that we gleaned from them seemed to make up for whatever the church lacked. When Elizabeth was born, she was included in the march to the podium with the other newborn babies to introduce her to the church. Our families attended, and we felt blessed. We still have that on video.

Over time, as Elizabeth got a little older, we needed to place her in the day care so we could attend services. Most of the time she did okay, but sometimes they couldn't handle her difficulties. It was always touch and go, and we were often on edge. The church overall seemed disorganized, with the left hand not knowing what the right hand was doing. The classrooms were always changing, and it was often difficult just to find out where to go. I filled out a card one time asking for prayer regarding my daughter's condition, as I discuss early in this book. As you'll recall, two young men and a young lady arrived at my door a few weeks later in response, but they had no idea exactly why they were there or what the issue was, and even though I invited them in, they quickly turned tail and left. As with our previous experience with Pastor Mike, they were focused entirely on money, sex, and salvation issues, none of which were our problems. At one point, the church had an autism class for children, but this disappeared. The kicker came when we wanted

Elizabeth to attend Vacation Bible School. We had her signed up, talked to the people involved, and felt it would be okay. But it wasn't. After a day, they asked us to come get her and not bring her back. They simply could not handle her. We were disappointed and despondent that such a large church with massive resources and large salaries for its staff did not have the ability to provide support for special-needs children. We figured it was time for a new church.

I think we visited just about every church in the area, big and small. A small church near our home seemed promising, as Elizabeth did well just sitting in the pews with me on several occasions. However, resources were limited in such a small church, and the sermons and regular Sunday service lacked the spiritual enrichment I was used to. My wife and I also liked more traditional services, with music from the Baptist hymnal. Now I know this is a controversial issue and is a matter of taste. I don't fault anyone for liking the concert-style services. However, I really feel like I'm worshipping the Lord most when I sing the traditional hymns. The hymns are easy for me to sing to, and they have a pomp and circumstance about them that seems fitting for praising the Lord. They remind me of my childhood church experience and give me a sense of tradition and continuity. More importantly, the focus of the singing is on the congregation. The concert style approach seems to focus more on the people singing on stage, much like a rock show. The songs are harder for some to sing to, and as a result, many people just listen. Many of the newer songs have an airy, melancholy quality about them that makes me sad. But this is just a matter of taste. If you like the concert-style music, don't let me dissuade you. Anyway, my wife and I wanted a church that had traditional music in some form, as either part of the main service or as an optional service, in addition to support for our child's needs.

While driving home from my office one day I noticed a sign outside of a church that I had passed by a few times. The sign was for something called SHINE, a program for special-needs children. The church was a big one but not nearly as huge as what we had been attending. I hurried home and told my wife about it. After reading up a little about this church on the Internet and making a couple of calls, we got in touch with the person who managed the program, and she was so helpful and kind. They had no problems taking Elizabeth on so we could attend services, and Elizabeth would get to attend the children's service too!

When we arrived, we met with the people managing the SHINE program and tried to figure out what would work best for Elizabeth. They tried taking her to a regular classroom with a buddy and then to a room to herself. What worked best for Elizabeth was having a buddy sit with her while she attended the "kid city" worship session with the other children. She loved it so much! Every Sunday she would be so excited about going to church, you'd think we were taking her to Disney World!

We found fulfillment as well. It was nice meeting people who had many of the same challenges we had. We joined a Sunday school class that had some nice people and an excellent teacher. The pastor's sermons were even better than what I had experienced at our previous church, and they even had an alternate service in the chapel with traditional music. We felt at home. There was no negativity or aloofness. During the new members' class, we sat with someone who was transferring from the same church we had gone to, and this person brought up some of the same issues—the disconnectedness, apathy, and lack of services despite it being such a large church with such a large budget. We knew then that it wasn't just us, that it was a problem with that church. We were certainly glad we had finally found our church home. Elizabeth was even able to attend Vacation Bible School for the first time, and when she came home, she could sing every part of "Jesus Loves Me." She had such a beautiful voice, and we felt so blessed. It brought tears to our eyes and still does to this day when I think about it.

I can't emphasize enough how important it is to find the right church. Don't get discouraged; the right one is out there for you. There are churches that have services for special-needs children; you just have to get out there and find them. My wife and I have been so blessed and enriched by this church that we could not imagine going anywhere else. We truly believe and feel that this is where the Lord wants us, and we're here to stay. Once you find that right church, get involved! You'll be even more blessed as a result.

To close this chapter, I'll leave off with two importance Bible passages:

But be doers of the word, and not hearers only, deceiving yourselves. For if anyone is a hearer of the word and not a doer, he is like a man who looks intently at his natural face in a mirror. For he looks at himself and goes away and at once forgets what he was like. But the one who looks into the perfect law, the law of liberty, and perseveres, being no hearer who forgets but a doer who acts, he will be blessed in his doing. If anyone thinks he is religious and does not bridle his tongue but deceives his heart, this person's religion is worthless. (James 1:22–27)

And let us consider how to stir up one another to love and good works, not neglecting to meet together, as is the habit of some, but encouraging one another, and all the more as you see the Day drawing near. (Hebrews 10:24–25)

19

Elizabeth's Singing

Not long after Elizabeth was first diagnosed, we got her into music therapy. We also had her in occupational, physical, speech, and ABA therapies at the time, but it seemed that she enjoyed the music therapy most. I think music is an excellent way to help improve speech and attentiveness in autistic children. It also gives them an activity they enjoy. Not only does Elizabeth love listening to music, but she also loves playing some instruments as well. Elizabeth cannot play songs, but she tries to follow along with the beat if she has a drum or tap on a xylophone or piano.

The most astonishing development out of music therapy was Elizabeth's voice. Elizabeth developed a fantastic ability to sing, with a great vibrato. Her voice can have a professional sound to it when she wants it to. I have had several hours of singing lessons, and the best I can ever do is carry a tune, but I still cannot add a good vibrato to my voice as a singer should. With Elizabeth, it comes naturally, but I don't think she would have developed it without help from music therapy.

We have kept Elizabeth in music therapy since she was a tot, and she thoroughly enjoys it. Most providers also hold music camps during the summer months, which I also highly recommend.

We believe that singing is a talent for Elizabeth, and we want to develop it. Music therapy is a vital part of making that happen for her, and it could be something your child would gravitate to as well. Perhaps it's not singing, but maybe piano or other instruments would turn on a special talent in your child. Artwork is another possibility. It's a wondrous thing. The Bible has much to say about activating such gifts:

> Oh come, let us sing to the LORD; let us make a joyful noise to the rock of our salvation! (Psalm 95:1)

> About midnight Paul and Silas were praying and singing hymns to God, and the prisoners were listening to them. (Acts 16:25)

> Having gifts that differ according to the grace given to us, let us use them: if prophecy, in proportion to our faith. (Romans 12:6)

I encourage every parent of a special-needs child to constantly find ways to expose your child to different stimuli. Your child has a talent or special strength that is waiting to be brought out, and you never know how or when that will happen, so try everything!

That said, the kind of therapists and providers you set your child up with can be critical, so you need to pay close attention to what they are doing and what you are getting for your money. Unfortunately, a lot of therapists tend to be rather transient, so when you find someone who is good for your child, it's hard to keep the same person for very long before the therapist quits or moves out of town.

In the beginning, your therapist may focus on playing instruments and doing sing-alongs. If a talent or interest seems to emerge at home in a special area, such as with an instrument, ask the therapist to focus on that a bit more and integrate it more readily into the sessions. Most therapists are pretty good about this, but sometimes it takes a nudge from the parents to influence the curriculum. Be sure not to position your request in such a way as to make it look like you are asking for music or singing "lessons," because they will balk at that. Focus on the therapeutic aspects: "She gets a lot out of this particular instrument" or "We've seen a lot of progress in her speech since she's done a lot of singing; her voice sounds so much clearer," etc.

There can also be problems with billing. Insurance can be flaky about covering music therapy, but a good medical billing specialist can make it happen. This is a common point of frustration for both parents and providers. Many providers don't like to handle insurance and just want parents to pay up, but few parents can afford the cost out-of-pocket without insurance picking up at least part of the bill. Since most children in this situation have numerous other therapies going on, music therapy is often the first to be cut and the last to be paid. This is a shame, but it is reality. Many therapy houses simply believe that billing is not their job and that they should focus on therapy alone, but the truth is that billing is part of the business. If they know their business well, they should have a good billing and insurance administrator on staff who knows how to navigate insurance challenges. This is often a good indicator of how well the business is run overall. Just like that old adage that says if you want to know how clean a restaurant is, take a look at the bathrooms, few providers can do insurance billing well, but if they do, you can be assured they have their act together in other ways.

Lessons Learned

1. Explore music therapy with your autistic child. He or she may take to some aspect of it, or he or she may not, but it's worth a try.
2. Try to find a good provider, and stick with this provider. This is easier said than done, but keep trying.
3. Work closely with your insurance company and provider on billing. It can be a lot of work for what is perceived by some as a low-priority service, but if your child is really benefiting from it as ours has, it is worth the trouble.
4. Observe and influence your child's curriculum. Ask for regular updates, and get providers to focus on what you think your child is benefiting from most. Ask for their feedback as well; after all, they are supposed to be the experts.
5. Your child has a special talent. I believe all children do. It may not be in music; it could be art or something entirely different. But you'll never find out God's plan if you don't explore and pray!

20

Elizabeth's Love and Sweet Spirit

The media's impression of an autistic child is typically one who is incommunicative, devoid of emotion, and often even tormented. I can see how some people unfamiliar with autistic children may have this impression after watching them have a tantrum in the mall or throw a fit at the grocery store. But as parents we know it's not always like that, and as the children get older, it *does* get better. When Elizabeth was little she was more fretful and had tantrums more often. Getting her gut calmed down along with finding her proper therapy made a big difference. Prayer helps too! Don't ignore your own spiritual well being!

Elizabeth has turned out to be a loving, spirited, and happy child. Most of our time is spent playing and enjoying her company. She sings songs, including everything from nursery rhymes to spirituals. She is full of love for us and compassion for others.

Can Autistic Children Show Love?

I've been asked this question before. Yes, they certainly can and do! Elizabeth will hug, pet, and coo around us to show affection. She didn't always do this, but it changed as she got older. In fact, the older she has gotten, the more affectionate she has become. She doesn't always say it in words, but she shows love with her gestures, smiles, and her eyes. Her big blue eyes are filled with a sweet spirit. She's at that stage of childhood where parents are still "cool," and she wants nothing more than to be with and around us. She shows compassion and love for others too; if she sees another child or baby, she will approach, pat the child with affection, and try to communicate with the child in some way.

Elizabeth wants the same things as other kids—attention, affection, and approval. If we ignore her, she gets mad. If we are unhappy with something she's done, she begs for forgiveness. If we get excited about her accomplishments, she hops with joy! Whenever Debbie and I become upset with each other, Elizabeth is upset too. She shares our emotions and our lives, just as any other child would.

Are autistic children unhappy or always tormented? No. In fact, nothing could be further from the truth. Yes, they have their bad moments, but so does a typical child. Elizabeth's bad moments may be different; she may have a few more of them because of her challenges, but the successes far outweigh the failures. The happy times are more frequent than the bad. Yes, it *does* get better as the child gets older and you become used to his or her unique habits. Treatments and prayer do work as well. As the Bible says, "Behold, children are a heritage from the Lord, the fruit of the womb a reward" (Psalm 127:3).

A few things are for sure: Elizabeth has a sweet soul, God has put her in our lives for a purpose, and it's a joy knowing that we are living God's plan. As the Bible teaches, we aim to have joyful hearts: "A joyful heart is good medicine, but a crushed spirit dries up the bones" (Proverbs 17:22).

21

God Has a Plan

If there's one thing I'm sure about, it's that God has a plan for Elizabeth. The future of our special children is something we all struggle with. Understanding why God allows such seemingly tragic things happen to good people is one of the perennial conflicts that many have with religion. First and foremost, we must understand that God's wisdom is infinite and beyond our understanding. Second, if the world were perfect and there were no suffering, would people still worship God? Would they still get down on their knees and plead for forgiveness of their sins? Not likely. In many ways, God lets bad things happen to remind us all that we are *not God* and that we must fear and worship *him*. For you can bet that if there were no suffering here on earth, people would probably worship themselves or some other entity, if anything. Certainly they would not worship God. The Bible teaches us to appreciate suffering: "More than that, we rejoice in our sufferings, knowing that suffering produces endurance, and endurance produces character, and character produces hope, and hope does not put us to shame, because God's love has been poured into our hearts through the Holy Spirit who has been given to us" (Romans 5:3–5).

What We Have Learned from Elizabeth

With our special children, our godly understanding can be expanded even further. They are indeed a gift. It may take time to understand that gift, but it is there, and it may not be in the way you would expect.

Elizabeth shows talents for singing and music. She is also a very smart girl, and her receptive language is, as far as we can tell, typical. She understands everything that goes on around her. By far, the most telling contribution that Elizabeth is making is her impact on our lives. She has brought to our home a love like my wife and I have never known. She has enriched us with laughter and joy but also tears. She has taught us how to see the best in others, no matter how beset by problems they may be. She has helped us find a church home and brought us closer to it and to the Lord. She has taught us empathy. I no longer see special-needs children or disabled people the way I used to. I've learned not to discount such people. I've learned they have just as much value as the rest of us and in many ways do and think just as well as we do. They may have challenges that we don't have, but they have talents and gifts that we don't have, and they have the right to pursue those just as everyone else does. I've learned not to prejudge such people and to give them the benefit of the doubt. Their surprising talents and gifts will often far outweigh any challenges they have. In this way, we can see one of the true miracles of God. He uses such people to show us what the human spirit can do with his help. Where would we be without such miracles? It is indeed a miracle to see a person with missing limbs accomplish acrobatic feats or a blind person play the piano like a virtuoso. Even as "typical" or "healthy" people, we have challenges—just different ones. Everyone on this earth has his or her own struggle or fight to contend with. As the Bible teaches, "Count it all joy, my brothers, when you meet trials of various kinds, for you know that the testing of your faith produces steadfastness. And let steadfastness have its full effect, that you may be perfect and complete, lacking in nothing" (James 1:2–4).

In short, Elizabeth has taught us to be better people. I am a better human, citizen, and Christian because of her. I have grown and matured in ways that many people my age and older have not. I am a stronger person with even greater faith. Debbie and I were childless for eight years. During that time, we did a lot of things together. We traveled, went out in the evenings whenever we wanted, and had total freedom. But we were missing something. Even though Elizabeth has special needs, she has brought something into our lives that we would never have had otherwise. I would not trade her for the world. As Romans 8:28

proclaims, "And we know that for those who love God all things work together for good, for those who are called according to his purpose."

Yes, God has a plan for your child, even if that plan is to make *you* a better person or to lead *you* to God. If these happen, then your child has accomplished God's goal.

22

Taking Care of Yourself

fly a lot for my job, so I'm accustomed to hearing those same phrases and instructions that each passenger is supposed to listen carefully to while pulling out laptops or sending texts to loved ones before the plane takes off. Airlines have taken different approaches to these instructions to try to get people's attention; sometimes they even add comedy sketches or other attention-getting tricks. One instruction that has always stayed with me is the one about the oxygen masks. During one flight, the airline showed a video of a parent putting a mask on a child while the narrator said, "Be sure to put on your own mask before helping others." That always stuck with me, and it's not a selfish thing. When it comes to your child, the best chance he or she has for survival is *you*. You are the engine that keeps everything going, and if *you* go down, so does your child, because there won't be anyone else to pick your child back up. Most importantly, know that you are not alone in this struggle. In the Bible, 1 Peter 5:7–9 reads, "Casting all your anxieties on him, because he cares for you. Be sober-minded; be watchful. Your adversary the devil prowls around like a roaring lion, seeking someone to devour. Resist him, firm in your faith, knowing that the same kinds of suffering are being experienced by your brotherhood throughout the world."

During all the battles that we fought, my wife and I often forgot to take care of our relationship and ourselves. Taking care of a special-needs family member is taxing on everyone, especially the parents. It's draining and can cause conflict and fatigue. If you express this conflict in front of your child, it will make him or her feel even worse. Elizabeth, like many of these children, may not be able to express herself, but she understands much more than most realize. Autistic children know what's going on, and when you exhibit stress, it will affect them. As husband and wife, mother and father, try to support each other. When one is exhausted, the other should pick up the pieces and take over for a while. Be patient with each other's stress. Most of all, be sure to get out and have fun occasionally. If you can do that with your child, that's great. But there will be times when you can't, and you need time alone together to keep your relationship healthy. Here are some tips that will help:

1. Be sure to make time for each other, no matter what. Set aside time each week to go out, have fun, and just be alone together for a while.

2. Find at least two babysitters who are skilled in handling special-needs children. Your teachers at school could be a resource, and online services, such as Care.com, can be useful. We have two babysitters who are special-needs teachers. Our child does great with them, so much so that she looks forward to our evenings out as much as we do.

3. Maximize public services and other resources. Whether it's Medicaid, special-needs scholarships, summer camps, Babies Can't Wait, respite, or other services, be sure to take advantage of everything you can find.

4. Find activities that you all enjoy. I restore old cars and often tinker with them. I once bought a classic pickup truck and started fixing it up. Elizabeth loved the truck and would often look at it and pat it as she walked by. She'd say, "I want cars." She loved classic cars as much as I did. My wife also loved them. We started going for a ride every weekend in the old truck, and everyone had a great time. It was a way for us to bond as a family. We all relaxed and enjoyed our time together.

5. You need a vacation too. This can be tricky, because who can you find to babysit for several days in a row? If you decide to take your little one with you, will he or she tolerate the flight or car ride? This is where extended family can help. If they will donate their time and are willing, you are indeed blessed. If not, offering

payment of some kind, including transportation, is an option. Your mental health is important, so don't assign dollars to it if you can help it.

6. Become active in your church community. Your fellow congregants can be some of the most inspirational and loving people you will find.

23

Hope for the Future

We don't really know what the future holds for Elizabeth and our family. But does anyone? We could worry ourselves to death about whether she will reach adulthood and what will happen to her when she does, especially as my wife and I get older and have trouble even taking care of ourselves. But does any family know what the future holds for its members? How often do we read of families experiencing devastating tragedies that they had no way of predicting or preparing for? For example, when a teenage child with a promising future suddenly dies in a traffic accident or on the ball field, nobody expects such tragedy. It happens every day. All we can do is trust in the Lord that he will make a way for us: "Though the fig tree should not blossom, nor fruit be on the vines, the produce of the olive fail and the fields yield no food, the flock be cut off from the fold and there be no herd in the stalls, yet I will rejoice in the Lord; I will take joy in the God of my salvation. God, the Lord, is my strength; he makes my feet like the deer's; he makes me tread on my high places. To the choirmaster: with stringed instruments" (Habakkuk 3:17–19).

Trusting in the Lord and celebrating the little successes our children have are great ways to alleviate worry and, more importantly, help keep us sane! Be prepared for the future. Build a trust for your child, get him or her all needed services, and build relationships in your community that will pave the way for future assistance. But don't worry, because if you do, you will make yourself physically sick, which won't help your child at all. My wife and I both came down with severe stress-induced illnesses. If we hadn't become careful about managing our stress, these conditions could have become even more serious.

No one knows what the future holds, even "typical" families with healthy children. Tragedy can befall us all and almost always will, in some way, at some point. Remember the Bible's promise: "For the Lord will not cast off forever, but, though he cause grief, he will have compassion according to the abundance of his steadfast love; for he does not willingly afflict or grieve the children of men" (Lamentations 3:31–33).

The key is how we deal with it. Trusting in the Lord and getting active with your church family are the best resources available to help you cope with challenges today and tomorrow.

In the scriptures, Mary told one of her relatives, Elizabeth, of the miraculous birth of Jesus Christ. When Elizabeth heard the news, the baby in her own womb leaped for joy! This child would become known as John the Baptist. This passage is commonly referred to as "Elizabeth's song" because it is the first example of John the Baptist's ministry, as he testified to his own mother of the coming Messiah. Elizabeth's song is a spirit-filled response to Mary's news that God, in his grace, would send Jesus Christ for every believer. Elizabeth and her babe were filled with hope and happiness. It is this same hope and happiness that can belong to you and your special-needs child.

Elizabeth's Song

At that time Mary got ready and hurried to a town in the hill country of Judea, where she entered Zechariah's home and greeted Elizabeth. When Elizabeth heard Mary's greeting, the baby leaped in her womb, and Elizabeth was filled with the Holy Spirit. In a loud voice she exclaimed: "Blessed are you among women, and blessed is the child you will bear! But why am I so favored, that the mother of my LORD should come to me? As soon as the sound of your greeting reached my ears, the baby in my womb leaped for joy. Blessed is she who has believed that the LORD would fulfill his promises to her!" (Luke 1:39–45 NIV)

Have you given your life to Christ? As I mentioned earlier, we fought hard for Elizabeth and still do every day. I can't imagine being able to do that without my faith in Jesus Christ. If you have not, I urge you to purchase a Bible, begin reading, and visit a local Bible-based church. Start by reading the passages I have quoted in this book, and then move on to the related chapters. I believe you will find them enlightening. If you believe that Jesus Christ is the Son of God and that he died on the cross for your sins, pray this prayer right now. Confess your sins to God, and express your faith to him in Jesus Christ. Ask for forgiveness and to be saved. Once you have done that, get involved in a local church and get baptized. You will need to feed your soul every week to grow in your faith. There will always be challenges, successes, and failures, but the difference is that now you won't be alone. As it is written in Psalm 23:1–6, "The Lord is my shepherd; I shall not want. He makes me lie down in green pastures. He leads me beside still waters. He restores my soul. He leads me in paths of righteousness for his name's sake. Even though I walk through the valley of the shadow of death, I will fear no evil, for you are with me; your rod and your staff, they comfort me. You prepare a table before me in the presence of my enemies; you anoint my head with oil; my cup overflows."

Finally, don't be afraid to pray for love, healing, and support for your little one. *He* has a plan. We may not know what that is at first, but being saved and turning our lives over to *him* is the first step in discovering it. The Bible reminds us, "Do not be conformed to this world, but be transformed by the renewal of your mind, that by testing you may discern what is the will of God, what is good and acceptable and perfect" (Romans 12:2).

References

Attkisson, Sharyl. "Family to Receive $1.5M in First-Ever Vaccine-Autism Court Award." CBS News. September 10, 2010. Accessed December 28, 2017. https://www.cbsnews.com/news/family-to-receive-15m-plus-in-first-ever-vaccine-autism-court-award/.

Printed in the United States
By Bookmasters